HOW AMERICAN FOREIGN
POLICY IS MADE

HOW AMERICAN FOREIGN POLICY IS MADE

SECOND EDITION

John Spanier
University of Florida

Eric M. Uslaner
University of Maryland

Holt, Rinehart and Winston/Praeger
New York   Chicago   San Francisco   Dallas
Montreal   Toronto   London   Sydney

© 1978 by Praeger Publishers,
A Division of Holt, Rinehart and Winston
   All rights reserved.

Library of Congress in Publication Data

Spanier, John W
   How American foreign policy is made.
   Bibliography: p. 180
   Includes index.
   1. United States—Foreign relations administration.
I. Uslaner, Eric M., joint author. II. Title.
JX1706.A4 1978b   353.008'92   77-89739

ISBN 0-03-041831-3 pbk.

Printed in the United States of America

890   090   987654321

For
William Spanier
and in memory of
Liesel Spanier
and
Abe and Irene Uslaner

PREFACE

Much recent debate about what is good and what is bad in the American political system has centered on foreign policy questions. In spite of this, most recent books on the policy process focus on *domestic* policy-making. Critical questions about the making of foreign policy have been ignored or left to journalists and members of the executive and legislative branches or treated in specialized studies on foreign policy. *How American Foreign Policy Is Made* has been written to fill the need for an introduction to the actors and elements in the foreign policy decision process and to the analytic approaches most useful in understanding and criticizing it.

Contemporary conflict over foreign policy demanded, too, that we not only deal with the process of foreign policy-making but confront as well the question of whether the outcomes of this process can be both effective and democratic. To this end, we examine the variations in the constitutional and political power of the president and Congress in both domestic and foreign policy formation. We also examine the actual access to foreign policy decision roles of various possible participants, the parts that may be played by congressmen, parties, and interest groups, and the impact of the media and expressions of public opinion.

The rational-actor and bureaucratic models of decision-making are suggested as aids to clearer understanding of the interaction of all these forces. The utility of these models is demonstrated in three case studies: the Cuban missile crisis of 1962, the decision to mine Haiphong harbor in 1972, and the process of enacting ABM legislation in the Johnson and Nixon Administrations.

The recent past suggests that presidential dominance has become a "given" in American foreign policy-making, so our concluding chapter returns to the question: Can policy formulation be both effective and democratic? Drawing on American experience in World War II and the Korean and Vietnam wars, we ask: How might events have been altered by enlarged Congressional participation? Would the outcomes in fact have conformed to the democratic expectations of today's reformers?

These are complex issues, and we do not claim to have resolved them. Rather, our goal is more modest: to outline for the introductory student of American government or of American foreign policy the foreign policy-making process and to highlight the problems we believe are the most important. In any such endeavor, particularly a joint one, some arguments are bound to remain somewhat incomplete in the eyes of the specialist. Our problem was somewhat compounded by differing views on what would constitute a "good" foreign policy—and, indeed, on how much of a say Congress should have. Such disagreements have led us to produce balanced arguments on different sides of critical issues—and also to examine the feasibility of proposed reforms regardless of our personal biases. This is the focus of the final chapter.

Much has, of course, changed since the first edition of *How American Foreign Policy Is Made*. A president, facing imminent impeachment, resigned from office; the war in Vietnam came to an end, although in a manner which we could not predict at the time we wrote the first edition; and perhaps the major figure in American foreign policy, Secretary of State Henry Kissinger, joined the ranks of former government servants when an obscure peanut farmer beat the odds (and many better-known opponents) to win the Democratic nomination for president and then go on to defeat Gerald R. Ford for the nation's highest office. Now, we find ourselves returned to the pre-Nixon era, with many of the familiar faces of the Kennedy-Johnson years in office once again. However, we face a new set of problems and the foreign policy—domestic policy distinction which seemed somewhat (if not totally) clear to us a few years ago has become increasingly blurred.

We owe special debts of gratitude to our colleague, William G. Munselle, for his many helpful suggestions on the first edition. We are also grateful to Sam Postbrief and Cheryl Christensen, both of the University of Maryland–College Park, who were helpful on several key points, as well as Phillip Rourk of the University of Maryland–College Park who helped Uslaner in the research of several points. Finally, we wish to thank our editor Denise Rathbun, who, as before, was patient and extremely helpful in catching errors of both ommission and commission. We are also grateful to the Division of Research of the University of Florida Graduate School for its assistance in the typing of the manuscript.

J.S.
E.M.U.

CONTENTS

1

FOREIGN POLICY AND DECISION-MAKING: THE DEMOCRATIC DILEMMA

THE ISSUE OF PRESIDENTIAL POWER

The United States officially has one president, but he occupies two presidencies.[1] One deals with the domestic political system, the other with the international one. In domestic matters, it has always been considered vital to limit presidential power to preserve the constitutional design of American democracy. The nation's historical tradition has been one of fear and suspicion of concentrated power, whether it existed in the governmental or economic area. The possession of power has been equated with its potential abuse, and power was therefore domestically distributed vertically between the federal government and the states, and within the federal government it was separated horizontally among the executive, legislative, and judicial branches.

By contrast, the conduct of foreign policy—whose principal aim is safeguarding the nation's security so that its way of life at home may be preserved and enjoyed—requires a concentration of executive power. In the international, or state, system, in which each state is its own protector and must rely primarily upon its own resources and strength, it is the chief executive who is usually considered the defender of the "national interests." This was as true in the days before democracy, under the rule of the crown, as it is in contemporary democracies, authoritarian and totalitarian states. Survival in an essentially anarchical international system whose principal rule is self-help requires a single source of authority so that a state can, if necessary, act speedily, secretly, with continuity of purpose or, when demanded, with flexibility. From the beginning of the modern state system it was taken for granted that legislatures, especially as the democratic representatives of the people, were incapable of the serious conduct of foreign affairs; public opinion was felt to be too ignorant, too impassioned, and too unstable. Parliaments as legislative institutions were by their very nature thought to be incapable of rapid decisions; to pass wise legislation, they were expected to debate at some length and reconcile conflicting interests and viewpoints. In short, the primacy of the executive in foreign policy was essentially a response to the nature of the state system.

Because of the domestic system's requirements to restrain executive power and the state system's need for ample executive power, tension between the two U.S. presidencies is inevitable.[2] *On the one hand, if the president is limited sufficiently to protect American democracy the danger is that he might also become so enfeebled that he will not be able to effectively defend the nation's interests. On the other hand, if the president accumulates enough power to act with the necessary authority, dispatch, and secrecy to protect the nation he might become so powerful that he will erode the restraints on his power which were intended to preserve the constitutional nature of the American political system.* Thus what is a virtue domestically might become a vice internationally, as the nation falls victim to its democratic organization; and what is a virtue externally might become a vice internally, as the nation loses its democratic soul in seeking to protect its democratic order from foreign threats.

The conduct of foreign policy, therefore, poses a dilemma for American democracy: how to preserve a democratic order at home while investing the government with enough authority to effectively guard the nation's security. It was John Locke, significantly enough, who first wrote about this problem. Usually regarded as the theorist whose political philosophy underlay the Declaration of Independence and the Constitution, Locke asserted that man possessed certain natural or inalienable rights which in society would be protected by the election of representatives who, through the legislature, would restrain the executive from abusing these rights and undermining the democratic nature of society. Externally, however, nations continued to live in a "state of nature" with one another, and therefore the executive—whom in the conduct of foreign affairs Locke called the federative power—could not be similarly contained.

> These two powers, executive and federative, though they be really distinct in themselves, yet one comprehending the executive of the municipal laws of the society within itself . . . ; the other the management of the security and interests of the public without. . . . And though this federative power in the well or ill management of it be of great moment to the commonwealth, yet it is much less capable to be directed by antecedent, standing, positive laws than the executive; and so must necessarily be left to the prudence and wisdom of those whose hands it is in, to be managed in the public good.[3]

It was Locke, then, who first distinguished between the two presidencies—the executive and the federative—which are both embodied in one man: the president, situated at the crossroads where the domestic and international systems meet and overlap.

THE CONSTITUTION AND THE DEMOCRATIC DILEMMA

In an effort to strike a balance between the demands of the state system—or what Paul Seabury has called the "intrinsic authoritarian necessities of foreign affairs"[4]—and the democratic needs of the internal order, the framers of the U.S. Constitution vested exclusive responsibility for the conduct of foreign policy in the federal government and then divided its authority in this field, as in the domestic, between the president and Congress. The president could receive and send ambassadors—that is, deal with representatives of foreign powers—but the Senate had to give its consent to treaties by a two-thirds vote and confirm top diplomatic, military, and political appointments. The president was appointed commander-in-chief of the armed forces, but only Congress was empowered to declare war, appropriate funds for the maintenance of military forces, and regulate commerce with other nations. It could also investigate the operations of the various executive departments that participated in the formulation and implementation of the foreign policy of the United States.

Thus, while the sharing of the foreign policy power by separate institutions was to ensure a check on presidential power, the president clearly was constitutionally the nation's chief diplomat and commander-in-chief. But a number of changes in the social and economic environment increasingly upset the balance between the executive and legislative branches and shifted power toward the president. Most of these new conditions have affected the conduct of both foreign and domestic affairs in all nations, but particularly in those of the West. First, and perhaps most fundamental, is the general growth of Big Government—which has usually meant "executive government." Running a highly urbanized, complex, industrial society has required big government and large bureaucracies to serve its manifold needs. The mass vote and the mobilization of new groups and classes into the political process have multiplied demands upon government for services ranging from guaranteeing high employment, subsidies of all types, stabilization of the economy, and redistributing power and money in society to even such formerly private affairs as dispersing knowledge and means of birth control.

Presidents and prime ministers in the relatively open societies of the West, as leaders of political parties from whom the electorate expects the satisfaction of certain demands, have become the central figures; as heads of their party and government, they draw up the social and economic programs, as well as foreign policies, to be submitted to the legislature, and it becomes their responsibility to shepherd bills through Congress or Parliament. Legislatures do not as a matter of fact act on their own. They wait for the executive to submit his program. And it is upon this record of achievement that the parties and their leaders run in the next election and seek to renew their mandate to govern.

Even nations that are neither democratic nor economically developed share this global trend toward executive government. States that, like the Soviet Union, do not possess a constitutional tradition may have a legislature, but such a body has no independent status and power. The executive has complete authority and governs unchallenged. In the new, ex-colonial, economically underdeveloped countries, too, power is centralized in the executive to try and hold the new fragmentary nation together and organize its human and material resources for modernization. One-party governments and military regimes exist throughout the Third World; parliamentary bodies, with few exceptions, are in decay, if they still survive. Executive dominance, whether justified by efficiency, ideology, or impatience, has everywhere emerged as the way to ensure results.

In the case of the United States another obvious fact needs to be noted in this regard. The president is nationally elected, and he, more than any other figure, represents the national mood and is the spokesman for the nation's interests, domestic and foreign. Congress, on the other hand, represents local interests; its representatives in the House and "ambassadors from the states" in the Senate respond mainly to their constituents' interests. Thus, it is not unfair to say that the president is more representative than any single congressman or senator and no less representative than all of them together.[5] By contrast, in Great Britain elections are organized around the parties and their national platforms. One votes for a member of Parliament because he represents one of the parties whose leader, if the party wins, becomes prime minister. But, unlike in Britain, the U.S. chief executive is also chief of state. He is more than a partisan leader and chief of government. In short, when he occupies the office of the presidency, he becomes the symbol of national unity and can thus draw upon most citizens' patriotism and loyalty. In England, the monarch is chief of state and stands above politics and differences over public policy, while the prime minister is chief of government. Therefore a United States citizen may often feel politically schizophrenic, hating and loving the president at one and the same time (as a partisan and American). In England, the citizen can hate the prime minister and still love, respect, and feel patriotic about his king or queen, although a great first minister of the crown such as Churchill may elicit much the same feelings. Not surprisingly, though, a president combining these two functions is constantly in the limelight and has a large corps of media correspondents assigned to him.

Only the president can instantly communicate with the people. Television, especially, has done much to expand the president's powers, but even in the days before the widespread use of radio, Theodore Roosevelt referred to the White House as a "bully pulpit." And the people, in turn, look toward the president for everything from national defense to social justice. Harry Truman once said that the president is the lobbyist for all the people. As chief of state, whether receiving a distinguished foreign dignitary or visiting other nations, especially our principal adversaries, Russia and China, and our main allies, he is covered by the press and television cameras—and therefore he can remain first in his nation's eyes, if not always in its heart. All in all, foreign policy, with its wars, crises, and glamour, magnifies the public's awareness of the president's leading role and its need for his leadership.

Since World War II and the advent of the atomic era, the president's foreign policy role has reinforced his central role in government to the point where he is no longer merely the "first among equals"; rather, he is, as one writer has said of the English prime minister, the "sun around which planets revolve."[6] The Constitution gave the presidency specific grants of authority with a great potential for expansion. These grants, such as that of commander-in-chief, were written in such a way that they were open to future interpretations as circumstances changed. In a real sense, what was not said in the Constitution "proved ultimately more important than what was."[7] Often called the Constitution's "great silences," they gave presidents —especially strong presidents such as Lincoln, the two Roosevelts, Truman, Kennedy, Johnson, and Nixon—freedom to do what they thought needed to be done in unprecedented circumstances on behalf of the nation's interests as they defined these, and to test the powers and limits of the office.

There were, to put it simply, "missing powers" in the Constitution. For example, the Constitution did not say where the powers to recognize other states or to proclaim neutrality were located. If the president and Senate must cooperate in the negotiation and ratification of a treaty, did they both have to agree also when terminating a treaty? If Congress must declare war, does it also make peace? Who proclaims neutrality, the president because he is commander-in-chief, or Congress because of its authority to declare war and regulate commerce? One frequent manner of determining who exercises these powers has been to assume that the foreign affairs powers explicitly granted imply other powers: The president's power to appoint and receive ambassadors, for example, implies the power to recognize or withhold recognition from other states. The "implied powers" doctrine, however, leaves much room for struggles between the executive and legislative branches for control of the conduct of foreign affairs—as the former enhanced its powers, especially during this century. As Louis Henkin has noted, the powers specifically allocated to the president are so few that "a stranger reading the Constitution would get little inkling of such large presidential authority, for the powers explicitly vested in him are few and seem modest, far fewer and more modest than those bestowed upon Congress[8]. . . . It seems incredible that these few meager grants support the most powerful office in the world and the multi-varied, wide-flung web-work of foreign activity of the most powerful nation in the world."[9]

Thus we return to our question: Can a democratic American domestic order be reconciled with an executive powerful enough to safeguard the nations's security so that it can continue to enjoy its way of life? Former Senator Fulbright (D., Ark.), deploring the imbalance between the executive and legislative branches of government, is a pessimist. "I for one am fairly well convinced that neither constitutional government nor democratic freedoms can survive indefinitely in a country chronically at war [presumably the cold war], as America has been for the last three decades. Sooner or later, war will lead to dictatorship."[10] Has post-World War II American foreign policy—the means to protect the security of American democracy—subverted the very aims it was intended to serve? Let us take a closer look at some of the characteristics of the foreign policy process.

CHARACTERISTICS OF FOREIGN POLICY
DECISION-MAKING

The principal characteristics of decision-making in the foreign policy sphere may be summed up as follows:

1. The actors and processes of foreign policy decision-making differ for each of the two broad types of foreign policy decisions, crisis decisions and program policy decisions.

Crisis decisions usually involve an element of surprise. The leaders have not been anticipating a threat from a foreign power; when the threat does occur, they perceive the need for a quick response lest the situation deteriorate to the detriment of the nation's security. For this reason, crisis decisions are made by the small number of actors at the very top of the executive "policy-making machine."

Program policy decisions, on the other hand, tend to become almost routine from year to year. A program policy involves long-run goals and the means of attaining them. Examples of such policies include the defense budget, trade agreements, treaties, and foreign aid. Most program policies, although formulated by the president and the bureaucracies, involve money and thus require congressional approval. Because many actors must participate, these policies may take a relatively long time to reach a culmination. Furthermore, because program policies express continuing goals, they tend to be marked by stable sets of actors.

2. The foreign policy elite is a relatively small group located in the executive branch, primarily the political leadership and the professional officers of the principal foreign policy bureaucracies. More specifically, this includes the president (politically elected), special assistants on National Security Affairs, secretaries, under secretaries and assistant secretaries (political appointees), as well as senior professional officers of both the Departments of State and Defense and the Central Intelligence Agency. On a secondary level, there are the upper ranks of the Arms Control and Disarmament Agency, the United States Information Agency, and the Agency for International Development, as well as other departments and agencies that have an intermittent interest in specific foreign policy issues, such as the Department of the Treasury's interest in monetary policy.

3. Most foreign policy decisions are arrived at through bureaucratic politics, because most are program policy decisions.
Different bureaucracies have different perspectives and training for their professional staffs, a need to believe in and justify
their tasks, and an understandable need to enhance their prestige, budgets, and influence—the more so if they are convinced of the importance of their contribution to the nation's
security and well-being. The different departments and agencies, in short, may see the same problem differently, or even
focus on different parts of the same problem and, therefore,
come up with varying and conflicting policy recommendations. The result, on the one hand, is bureaucratic conflict; on
the other hand, the need to make a decision produces a "strain
toward agreement or consensus."[11] Policy, therefore, results
from a process of bargaining and compromising.

4. The central and key figure in the foreign policy process
is the president. Although noncrisis policy is largely the product of bureaucratic conflict, this does not mean—as models of
bureaucratic struggle often imply—that the president is
merely one player among many, one chief among many departmental chiefs. He is more than merely a first among
equals; he is by far the most important player.[12] He, after all,
appoints the chiefs; presumably to a large degree they reflect
his values and owe him, as well as their departments, a degree
of loyalty. They can be fired if they no longer serve the president's purposes. He can also "stack the deck" by assigning a
policy to a particular chief and department or set of men. If he
selects "hawks" to investigate whether to intervene militarily
in Vietnam, as Kennedy did, he is likely to receive a report
favoring intervention; had he chosen "doves" he would in all
probability have gotten back quite a different answer.

Moreover, many problems require the consideration of so
many elements—political, economic, social, and psychological
—that nowhere short of the presidential level can these factors
really be balanced off against one another and integrated into
an overall policy. But perhaps the most important factor—
particularly in an era in which presidents have grown increasingly fond of being their own secretaries of state—is that presidents will seize for themselves specific areas of policy (e.g.,
arms control) or policies (e.g., negotiating an end to the war in

Vietnam). "The ability of bureaucracies to independently establish policies is a function of presidential attention. Presidential attention is a function of presidential values. The chief executive involves himself in those areas which he determines to be important."[13] Bureaucratic power is thus to a large degree a function of presidential—and, even further, congressional and public—inattention. In practice this means bureaucracy plays its largest role in routine day-to-day matters, its smallest during crisis periods. In any event, the increasing competition for presidential attention and support in policy struggles makes the competition among departments all the fiercer.

5. Interest group representation, articulation, and pressure, while pervasive in domestic politics, are not nearly as extensive or intense in foreign policy. In this area groups tend to lack the interest, experience, and, above all, knowledge they possess on domestic issues. Two groups, the major economic and ethnic interests, are probably influential in foreign affairs to a limited extent on discrete issues. Business, agricultural, and shipping interests and labor organizations have a natural interest in trade, foreign investment, and tariff issues. And ethnic groups in a nation of immigrants have in the past often pressed for policies favorable to the former mother country; now that Germany and Italy are allies instead of enemies, however, the principal ethnic group with influence is the Jewish community, which has lobbied very successfully for American diplomatic, economic, and military support for Israel.

6. The public and Congress have been generally supportive of the president's conduct of foreign policy—at least until Vietnam. One reason is that most Americans simply are poorly informed and uninterested in foreign policy issues. Their knowledge and experience relate to affairs nearer home, such as family and professional life; the political opinions they do hold are more likely to be about national politics. At best policy-makers may sense a general mood, which may set broad limits on what they regard as feasible and permissible, but they do not receive specific operational cues. In general, it would be more accurate to say that public opinion on foreign policy is a response to the policy-makers' decisions and to public presentation of the issues.

Congressmen to a large extent have shared the average citizen's lack of familiarity and sense of incompetence on foreign affairs. Viewing them as esoteric matters beyond their personal experience, in contrast to farm or labor problems, confronted with expert civilian and military witnesses at committee hearings, they usually tend to subordinate their own presumed expertise—political judgment of the feasibility and acceptability of administration policies—to that of the president and his phalanx of bureaucratic help.

Thus, it is not understating the main difference between these two areas of policy to say that in the post-World War II era it has been easier for a president to intervene with military forces in faraway places than to cut social security benefits or farm subsidy programs. On issues of domestic policy, members of Congress feel that their judgments are sound and are based upon knowledge and experience. Consequently, the president has many strong adversaries and skillful competitors in the domestic policy struggles, and it is much more difficult for him to get his legislative program through Congress. Only on foreign policy can it be said that the president exercises the full scope of the powers of his office.

7. The role of parties in foreign policy has been defined in terms quite different from those applied to domestic policy by politicians themselves and by journalists and scholars. Largely stirred by the memory of the defeat of the Versailles Peace Treaty following World War I in the conflict between a Democratic president and a Republican Senate, the post-World War II assumption was that "politics should stop at the water's edge." Partisanship and the usual type of political considerations, it was held, had no place in the conduct of foreign affairs; here the national interest was to be placed ahead of party interest. In protecting the nation against external threats the president deserved the support of both parties. "Bipartisanship" became the new slogan and the patriotic thing to do; partisanship was to be confined strictly to domestic affairs. Executive-legislative hostility and party controversy over foreign policy might undermine the stability and continuity of U.S. policy, make it impossible to speak with one national voice in world affairs, and erode the nation's credibility in its dealing with friends and foes.

DOMESTIC AND FOREIGN POLICIES: THE QUESTION OF STAKES

A key element in any situation is how the various actors perceive the consequences of their actions. The differences between foreign and domestic policy-making are due, at least in part, to the different stakes involved and how the actors perceive them. In domestic policy-making, participants can often differentiate between the "winners" and the "losers." In foreign policy-making, on the other hand, the entire nation is usually seen as either "winning" or "losing." Most foreign policy decisions do not result in one group within the population gaining at the expense of others.* In domestic policy, the most clear-cut example of the winners-losers dichotomy may be the antipoverty program. This program is specifically designed to provide aid to an identifiable group in the population (the poor), who are classified as "losers" by such standards as income or housing. The poor are viewed as a "have-not" group, and the debate surrounding the antipoverty program is marked by arguments about what the government should do to aid disadvantaged groups at the expense (in taxes or prerogatives) of the "haves" in society—those people who have more or less "made it" in society. The goal, then, is to turn some of the "losers" into "winners."

On the broad questions of foreign policy, however, decisions are not generally viewed in terms of "winners" against "losers." Foreign policy decisions are more frequently viewed in terms of the entire country (rather than any particular group in the population) winning or losing. When a country goes to war, the winners and losers are the nations (or alliances) involved—not specific groups like the oil companies, the farmers, or the poor. Tensions within the country on domestic legislation are put aside as the population "rallies around the flag" in support of the president's actions as commander-in-chief.[14] Simply stated, the stakes are very different in foreign

*Not everybody sees foreign policy in this way. Notably, radical critics (on both the left and the right) do see foreign policy decisions as involving domestic winners and losers. Critics on the left, for example, may view foreign policy decision-making as a conflict between capitalists and the workers (just as they do in domestic politics).

and domestic politics. In domestic politics, there are a multitude of interest groups concerned with the decisions of government and attempting to influence them. Each group wants to be a winner rather than a loser or a nonwinner. Even though the president initiates more domestic legislation than does Congress, the chief executive's hands are tied to a much greater extent in domestic politics than in foreign politics. Groups and individuals looking out for their own interests attempt to influence Congress on how money should be spent, which tax loopholes should be closed or left untouched, and how business and labor should be regulated. The process of raising revenue and spending it for domestic programs is marked by a relatively high degree of conflict among the groups contending for special benefits. The mediating actors in domestic politics are Congress and the executive departments that draw up the federal budget. To some extent, the very large scope of the demands made can also serve to moderate these demands made by interest groups. The president simply cannot spend his time listening to all of these demands. He is willing in most cases to give up a large part of his power to Congress.

The situation is quite different in foreign policy. Since foreign policy decisions are not perceived either by the public or by the decision-makers as involving methods of "dividing up the spoils," the conflict over decisions made will involve a much smaller circle of actors. Interest groups become mobilized only when they see the potential to "win" something for themselves, but on most foreign policy issues either the entire country wins or the country loses. This is not to deny that some citizens or groups may differ vastly on foreign policy questions from other citizens or groups. But, significantly, each group views its own position as the one which is in the "national" (or even "international") interest.

The basic distinction, then, between conflicts over domestic and over foreign affairs concerns the way participants view the stakes of the policy process. On most domestic policies—and program policies in foreign policy such as the defense budget and reciprocal trade legislation—there are more likely to be winners and nonwinners than winners and losers. These pro-

gram policies, also called "distributive" policies, are "perceived to confer direct benefits upon one or more groups [but
are] determined with little or no conflict over the passage of
the legislation, but only over the size and specific distribution
of the shares."[15] On crisis decisions in foreign policy, however,
the whole nation either wins or loses, and the nature of the
conflict on such policies will be quite different. Conflict on
these crisis decisions is most likely to resemble the less frequent but loudly argued cases of domestic policies which propose to redistribute income from the "haves" in society to the
"have-nots," where again we see a clash between inevitable
winners and losers. Program policies thus involve many actors
who may have diverse goals and different perceptions of the
stakes involved. Crisis decisions, on the other hand, involve
only a small number of actors, and the stakes involved are
generally quite clear. Indeed, the high stakes involved in crisis
decisions are a key reason why the president is the dominant
actor in this area: The office of the presidency is the only actor
in the American political system capable of the swift and decisive action required in crises.

OF PRESIDENTS AND "INTERMESTIC" POLICY

Of the two presidencies, the foreign one is clearly the
stronger. In the domestic sphere the president has to bargain
harder and longer, and Congress, interest groups, and public
opinion are not as deferential and willing to accept presidential policies. To the extent that in policy the interest group
structure is relatively weak, public opinion permissive, and
Congress supportive, the executive will not only lead but have
a high degree of maneuverability, freedom to move whichever
way it wishes; conversely, the stronger these factors are, the
less discretion the policy-making elite possesses. Basically, this
distinction is equivalent to the difference between foreign and
domestic policy, although the distinction is by no means absolute. The autonomy allowed the chief executive in foreign
policy, of course, has immense attraction for him and since
1945 has reinforced his disposition to give foreign policy primary attention. He can more easily act on his own, receive
congressional assent, and thus emerge with a successful record,

a record which can benefit his party and reward the president with a place in history.

The presidential ability to gain legislative support in foreign and domestic policy has been summed up by one leading scholar of American politics as follows:

> The president's normal problem with domestic policy is to get congressional support for the programs he prefers. In foreign affairs, in contrast, he can almost always get support for policies that he believes will protect the nation—but his problem is to find a viable policy....
>
> In the realm of foreign policy there has not been a single major issue on which presidents, when they were serious and determined, have failed. The list of their victories is impressive: entry into the United Nations, the Marshall Plan, NATO, the Truman Doctrine, the decisions to stay out of Indochina in 1954 and to intervene in Vietnam in the 1960s, aid to Poland and Yugoslavia, the test-ban treaty, and many more. Serious setbacks to the president in controlling foreign policy are extraordinary and unusual.[16]

Omitting certain issues, such as immigration and refugees, which Congress considers as falling within its own jurisdiction, the record from 1948 to 1964, just before the massive American Vietnamese intervention, shows that presidents have prevailed 70 percent of the time on foreign and military issues in contrast to a 40 percent record on domestic issues. Thus, it seems clear that the president and the policy-making elite not only make the key decisions but to a large extent also mold public and congressional opinion; and this record has not essentially changed in recent years even though Congress since the Vietnamese debacle has become somewhat more assertive and examines executive policy proposals more critically.

What has, however, eroded increasingly is the distinction between foreign and domestic policy as a "new" kind of foreign policy has arisen. The former or "older" type of foreign policy has generally been conceived to deal with a state's security. In an international system which is basically anarchical each state is its own guardian. Viewing each other as potential adversaries, states rarely forget that the basic rule is to protect yourself. A lapse of memory is to risk endangering one's territorial integrity and political independence. The principal mechanism to ensure one's safety is the balance of power. If one state matches another state in strength, neither is likely to attack the other; but an imbalance may entice the stronger one to attack. Consequently, in the state system, in which each state sees an increase in power and security for another state as a loss of power and security for itself—a loss which it regards as unacceptable—preserving the balance of power constitutes the heart of its foreign policy. American foreign policy since World War II has therefore been concerned with the central balance with its principal adversary, the Soviet Union, and a series of regional balances in Europe, Asia, and the Middle East. Thus, the United States is involved in virtually every area of the world with many different nations as adversaries, allies, and nonaligned states.

The "new" foreign policy, of which states have become very conscious since 1973, and the quadrupling of oil prices by the Oil Producing Exporting Countries (OPEC), revolve around economic issues such as natural resources, especially energy, food, and population, and what is generally referred to as the widening gap between the rich or developed and poor or underdeveloped nations. A nation's welfare—even its security —can be undermined if, for example, an underdeveloped country possessing a vital resource such as oil needed by an industrial country withholds that resource or dramatically raises the price. OPEC's 1973 price increase has lowered Western living standards (as the same amount of money must be stretched for the higher cost of heating, air conditioning, transportation, and oil-based products from clothes to records), increased inflation, precipitated the worst Western recession since the 1930s, made it more difficult to resume a rapid rate of economic growth, and posed a danger for the social peace and political stability which had been based on a growing economic "pie" and the expectation of all social groups for increased prosperity. As they import more oil, the economic lives of these industrial societies have become increasingly dependent on their external sources—some live on the verge of bankruptcy—and since the nations most dependent on importing oil are America's allies in Western Europe and Japan, the security of all the democracies is endangered as well. Thus, the price of foreign oil suddenly became very much a domestic issue, as well as a foreign policy issue. Conversely, in a world of underdeveloped countries with a rapidly growing population whose feeding depends on an oil-based, high technology domestic farming plus imports from the West in years of shortages, and of repeated large Soviet demands for grain, food has also become intertwined with foreign policy. American food exports now earn much of the money needed to pay for OPEC oil; it can be used to advance political purposes (e.g., to bolster detente with Russia or provide Egypt with an incentive to orient her foreign policy toward the United States), and, in cases of starvation, for humanitarian aims. As American consumers compete for food with Indians and Russians, United States food prices, already raised by the higher price of oil, rise further.

Thus there is a new class of policies which has been called "intermestic",[17] a mixture of inter(national) and (do)mestic policies. This is because these policies in which nations are said to be increasingly linked together economically—hence, in the frequently used phrase, are "interdependent" so that a disruption of supplies or a major price change can dislocate entire economies and affect tens of millions of people—span both arenas. Whether the origin of the policy is external but spills over into the domestic arena, as in oil, or internal but spills over into the external arena, as in food, the domestic impact is profound. Unlike most security policies, with the major exception of war, these economic policies arouse all the actors domestic policies usually do: the executive agencies whose jurisdiction is domestic, interest groups, Congress, and public opinion. The State Department, articulating the "national interest," will hardly be heard above the din of voices of the Departments of Treasury, Agriculture, and Commerce, their respective congressional committees, and the clientele or interest groups in each of these and other policy areas, all of whom feel expert in these areas, possess major stakes and can articulate their viewpoints, and usually have a good deal of "clout" since they represent specific, well-organized and financed groups who normally represent millions of voters. As a result of the active involvement of all these actors, the president's ability to initiate, lead, and maneuver will, as in domestic policies in general, be more constrained than on security issues. Thus, it is possible both to say that "foreign policy is made in a different way than domestic policy" and "foreign policy is made in the same way as domestic policy." If this is a paradox, it is because these are two different kinds of foreign policies, one in the security area and the other in the economic area.

2

PRESIDENTIAL PREEMINENCE
IN THE MAKING
OF FOREIGN POLICY

PRESIDENTIAL PREOCCUPATION WITH FOREIGN AFFAIRS

The preeminence of presidents in the domain of foreign policy is visible in the names attached to specific policies: Washington's Farewell Address, Jefferson's Embargo, the Monroe Doctrine, Theodore Roosevelt's "Big Stick," Wilson's Fourteen Points, Franklin Roosevelt's Good Neighbor Policy, the Truman Doctrine, the Eisenhower Doctrine, and—inevitably—the Nixon Doctrine. President Nixon in 1970 even began issuing an annual State of the World message to supplement the yearly State of the Union message. The latter formerly included a president's assessments and general recommendations on foreign and domestic policies; Nixon separated the two. Indeed, Jimmy Carter's "human rights" campaign has become the dominant theme of his administration, the cornerstone of foreign policy decision-making as perceived by both domestic and foreign observers. To a greater extent than other presidents, Carter has sought the involvement of the American public as well as friendly foreign leaders in stressing the need to extend basic civil liberties as widely as possible.

In retrospect, it is somewhat surprising that earlier presidents did not issue a separate foreign policy report. Since the end of World War II, most of our presidents have been primarily interested and concerned with foreign policy issues. Truman had little choice; circumstances made it necessary for him to give most of his time to foreign policy and, having chosen excellent advisers, he will be remembered by history primarily as a great or near-great president for his foreign policy. President Eisenhower, the general who had led Allied armies to victory in Europe, was elected during the frustrations of Nationalist China's collapse and the protracted Korean War, which he promised to end. John Kennedy left no doubt that he sought his fame and reputation by his handling of foreign policy; in his inaugural address he confidently asserted that the United States "shall pay any price, bear any burden, meet any hardship, support any friend, oppose any foe to assure the survival and the success of liberty."[1] President Nixon, too, clearly considered foreign policy his particular area of expertise and showed far less interest in domestic affairs. Before his inauguration, he was quoted as saying that the country needed a president for the conduct of foreign policy; the cabinet could take care of domestic policies. His reorientation of American policy toward Communist China and his negotiations with Russia on a broad front from arms control to trade preoccupied the president in his attempt to lay the foundation of a "generation of peace."

By contrast, President Johnson's fate tragically symbolized the plight of a president whose principal experience was domestic and whose fundamental wish was to enact a social reform program to rival that of his mentor, Franklin Roosevelt. Unfortunately the world would not go away. Thus Johnson, upon succeeding President Kennedy after the latter's assassination, pushed more liberal social legislation through Congress than any president in the twentieth century, including Franklin Roosevelt. But foreign policy proved his undoing. Vietnam not only forced him from office in 1968 but has seemingly stained his historical reputation.

One result of the trend toward concentration on foreign affairs has been that presidents have also increasingly become their own secretaries of state. Wilson set the precedent; he clearly overshadowed William Jennings Bryan, the former Democratic presidential candidate and great orator, as well as Bryan's successor, Lansing. Franklin Roosevelt hardly even paid any attention to his secretary of state, Cordell Hull. During World War II, in his meetings with Prime Minister Churchill and Premier Stalin, he usually left Hull at home and uninformed. Kennedy deliberately selected a relatively weak secretary of state, Dean Rusk, and Nixon from 1969 to 1973 chose a friend, William Rogers, who, unlike Rusk, had no experience in foreign affairs at all. Only Truman and Eisenhower had strong secretaries of state, Acheson and Dulles, respectively; and Nixon too, after Rogers, chose his foreign policy adviser, Henry Kissinger, a strong figure.

As presidents have more and more become their own secretaries of state, they have increasingly relied upon a personal adviser who, starting with Kennedy, came to be called a special assistant on National Security Affairs. Wilson had his Colonel House, and Franklin Roosevelt his Harry Hopkins. Kennedy appointed McGeorge Bundy from Harvard; Johnson, Walt Rostow from MIT; and Nixon chose Kissinger, also from Harvard. Under Nixon the position became institutionalized, and a sizable foreign policy staff under Kissinger's direction was assembled in the White House. This marks perhaps better than anything else the shift of the locus of foreign policy decision-making to the White House. Even when appointed secretary of state, Kissinger kept his White House position until the Congress in 1976 forced the controversial secretary to give up his position as National Security adviser to Nixon's replacement, Ford. Yet, the new security adviser was General Brent Snowcroft, Kissinger's deputy. Carter followed the traditional pattern of employing an academic adviser on foreign policy, Zbigniew Brzezinski of Columbia. Brzezinski had been one of Carter's chief advisers during his presidential campaign, but the centralization of power on foreign policy during the Nixon and Ford Administrations was one of Carter's principal campaign issues in 1976: He referred to the personal diplomacy conducted by Kissinger with foreign chiefs of state as the actions of the "Lone Ranger." Carter often acted as his own chief spokesman on foreign policy, but the institutional role of the State Department was restored to its prior role under Secretary Cyrus Vance. Unlike previous administrations, however, there was a history of good relations between Vance and Brzezinski, who had worked together both in and out of government.

TABLE 2-1. Major Party Presidential and Vice-presidential Candidates, 1952–76

Year	Presidential		Vice Presidential	
1952 DEM.	Stevenson*		Sparkman	Sen. F.R.
	Kefauver	Sen. A.S.		
	Barkley	Sen. F.R.		
	Russell	Sen. A.S. (Chairman)		
	Harriman	Sec. of Commerce and Committee on Foreign Aid (in executive to evaluate U.S. capability for Marshall Plan aid)		
1952 REP.	Eisenhower		Nixon	House Un-American, Select Com. Foreign Aid, 80th Congress
	Taft			
1956 DEM.	Stevenson		Kefauver	See 1952
	Harriman	See 1952	Kennedy	Sen. Gov't. Operations
	Kefauver		Humphrey	Sen. F.R.
1956 REP.	Eisenhower		Nixon	See 1952
			Stassen	Disarmament adviser
1960 DEM.	Kennedy	Sen. F.R.	Johnson	Sen. A.S.
	Humphrey	Sen. F.R.		
	Johnson	Sen. A.S.		
	Symington	Sen. A.S.		
1960 REP.	Nixon	See 1952	Lodge	Sen. F.R. 80th U.S. Ambassador to U.N.
	Goldwater			
	Rockefeller			
1964 DEM.	Johnson	See 1960	Humphrey	See 1960
1964 REP.	Goldwater	Sen. A.S.	Miller	
	Scranton			
	Rockefeller			
	Romney			
	Lodge	See 1960		

TABLE 2-1.   (Continued)

Year	Presidential		Vice Presidential	
1968 DEM.	*Humphrey* McCarthy R. Kennedy McGovern	See 1960 Sen. F.R. Director, Food for Peace	*Muskie*	Sen. Gov't. Operations
1968 REP.	*Nixon* Romney Rockefeller Reagan	See 1952	*Agnew*	
1972 DEM.	*McGovern* Muskie Humphrey Jackson Wallace Lindsay	See 1968 Sen. F.R. See 1960 Sen. A.S.	*Shriver* Eagleton	Director, Peace Corps
1972 REP.	*Nixon*	See 1952	*Agnew*	
1976 DEM.	*Carter* Brown Church Udall Jackson Wallace	Sen. F.R. Select Sen. Intelligence, chairman See 1972	*Mondale*	Select Sen. Intelligence
1976 REP.	*Ford* Reagan		*Dole* Schweiker	Select Sen. Intelligence

*Party nominees in italics; F.R. = Foreign Relations Committee; A.S. = Armed Services Committee.

Paralleling these developments in the post-World War II period has been a change in the pattern of recruitment of presidential candidates. Whereas Wilson, Harding, Coolidge, and Roosevelt in the interwar period had been governors, positions in which they gained experience in dealing with the problems of pre-Depression domestic America, all but two of the presidents since 1945 have come from the Senate. At a time when the United States was one of the two leading powers in the world, when nuclear weapons meant the deaths of tens of millions of Americans if war erupted (President Kennedy once estimated the count to be 100 million Americans, 100 million Europeans, and 100 million Russians), this is not really surprising. The expertise for dealing with these key issues of war and peace was in Washington, not state capitals. And in Washington, the Senate is the senior legislative body and is more involved in foreign policy-making than the House. Thus the emergence of the Senate as a launching platform for presidential candidates is natural. Truman was a senator, although he was not selected by Roosevelt as vice-president in 1944 because of his knowledge of foreign affairs. But what is very striking about post-Truman presidential and vice-presidential candidates—especially the winners of each nomination in both parties—is (1) the predominanace of U. S. senators and (2) membership of those senators in either the Foreign Relations Committee or the Armed Services Committee, with a slight edge for the former. The standout exception was Eisenhower, a military officer and public servant with much experience in foreign policy and diplomacy.

Two senators who were unsuccessful in their first tries for a place on their parties' national tickets and were successful the second time had in the interim become members of the key Senate committees. John Kennedy (D., Mass.) in 1956 was a member of the Senate Government Operations Committee when he sought the Democratic vice-presidency; four years later, when he became his party's presidential nominee, he was on the Foreign Relations Committee. Barry Goldwater (R., Ariz.), unsuccessful in 1960, was successful in 1964 and had in the meantime become a Senate Armed Services Committee member. Edmund Muskie (D., Me.), the Democratic vice-presidential candidate in 1968, joined Foreign Relations before the next election, when in the early going he was considered the front-runner for the Democratic presidential nomination.

Governors were generally unsuccessful, with the notable exception of Carter who had served as chief executive of Georgia from 1971 to 1975. There were two other governors who were nominated for president after World War II, Dewey in 1948 and Stevenson in 1952 and 1956. All three did have some experience and interest in foreign policy. Indeed, most of the state executives who have made serious presidential bids —including Nelson Rockefeller, William Scranton, and W. Averell Harriman—had foreign policy experience. Other governors did not even have the honor to lose the presidential contest for their party: they were not nominated. A state's chief executive who demonstrates an interest in foreign policy but also an inability to handle international problems may even be worse off than a governor who stresses domestic concerns almost to the exclusion of foreign policy. A case in point is former Michigan Governor George Romney. Romney was considered the front-runner for the Republican nomination in 1968 until he stated that the Johnson Administration had succeeded in "brainwashing" him on the proper course of action in Vietnam. The charge backfired on Romney, who appeared to many to be too gullible on any policy.

In contrast, Carter's foreign policy background was not an issue in a campaign based largely on domestic issues. The former Georgia governor had served as a member of the bipartisan Trilateral Commission, a foreign policy study commission headed by David Rockefeller, whose members also included Vance and Brzezinski. The purpose of this commission was to bring about closer political and economic relations among the industrial nations of Western Europe, the United States, and Japan. More critically, however, Carter was perceived as the "winner" (in terms of public opinion) on the televised debate with President Ford on foreign policy during the 1976 campaign. Even though Ford had "won" the domestic policy debate, the supposed area of Carter's strength, the strong performance of the challenger on the foreign policy forum established the candidate as a credible potential president to many voters. While Romney's blunder eliminated him from

the 1968 race, Carter's positive impression helped to restore
the momentum that the Democratic candidate seemed to
have lost. In any event, 1976 was the year of the greatest
recession and unemployment since the Great Depression and
the first president election since Vietnam and Watergate and
the general public mood of disillusion about an extensive foreign policy role and political institutions and politicians. In
1976, 27 percent of Americans over 18 voted for Carter, 26
percent for Ford while 47 percent stayed home; it was a year
in which the electorate for the first time in years showed that
most voters looked for new ideas rather than experience and
were very worried about the economy. Despite Carter's nomination and election in 1976, the fact remains that only one
other governor actually was elected on a national ticket in the
postwar years—Spiro T. Agnew in 1968 and 1972. Agnew, who
had not aspired to the post, was rather surprised at being
selected by candidate Nixon in 1968 to balance the GOP ticket
both geographically and ideologically. Both Nixon and Agnew,
of course, left office involuntarily; Agnew was replaced by another former governor, Nelson Rockefeller. However, Rockefeller had considerable foreign policy experience (indeed, he
introduced Kissinger to national political life) and, at the time
of his nomination, was serving as the head of a self-financed
research organization analyzing both foreign and domestic
policy alternatives.

Since Truman, presidents have also become so involved with
foreign policy problems, and especially crises when the fear of
nuclear war became especially acute, that at least until Vietnam domestic problems were bound to suffer neglect. The fact
that there are only so many hours per day and that the president can pay attention to only some of the many problems that
he should deal with, had he unlimited time, means that he has
to make a choice, and when the external danger is perceived
as high by the president and his advisers, foreign policy will
preoccupy them. Since throughout most of the post-1945 period the threat from Russia and China was seen as global in
scope, it is not surprising that domestic affairs were assigned to
a secondary status. One analyst has even asserted that "foreign
policy concerns tended to drive out domestic policy."[2] Indeed,
in a situation where even potential foreign crises like Vietnam

did not receive sufficient attention, and therefore tended to blow up into full-fledged crises, domestic affairs often seemed to gain consideration only when they too became critical. Sometimes, in fact, it appeared as if only domestic violence would attract sufficient attention and bring results, as, for example, when black rioting, burning, and looting dramatically demonstrated the frustration and anger among American blacks at their status and treatment 100 years after the Emancipation Proclamation.

This subordination of domestic to foreign policy has occurred with increasing frequency during this century, as the world more and more has been unwilling to leave America alone to attend to its domestic needs. Every president who has come into office bent on reform at home has sooner or later found himself confronted by external threats, which came to preoccupy his attention and led to the neglect of domestic problems. Wilson's New Freedom program was overtaken by the German menace and World War I; Franklin Roosevelt, or "Dr. New Deal," as he called himself, became "Dr. Win-the-War" early in his third term, as Hitler, Mussolini and Tojo made it impossible to complete domestic reforms; after 1945 Truman's Fair Deal quickly became subordinated to containment; Kennedy's New Frontier became a victim of one foreign crisis after another; and Johnson's Great Society was devoured by Vietnam.

This does not mean that, without the appearance and perception of external threats, presidents supported by Congress would have spent the resources used up by recurrent military preparations on domestic problems and reforms of various kinds. Roosevelt's New Deal program was stalled in Congress by 1938. Truman's Fair Deal made modest progress in 1949–1950, but was overshadowed by congressional criticism of the Korean War in the last two years of his administration. Eisenhower had no social program to speak of, and Kennedy's New Frontier remained largely rhetoric since Congress wanted no part of it. Johnson's Great Society was the exception, and it was made possible by the exceptional cricumstances of his immense persuasive skills, a landslide presidential victory that also elected a sizable number of Democratic congressmen, and the president's concentration on the enactment of his social legislation while trying to conduct the escalating Vietnam War in a "business as usual" atmosphere that demanded no sacrifices from the American people. This strategy worked until the 1966 mid-term election and the recapture by the Republicans of many of their former House seats. Nixon, in his turn, had few domestic interests except to dismantle much of his predecessor's social programs. Thus, the lack of social reform between Roosevelt's second term and Johnson's succession after Kennedy's assassination is due in large part to the conservative and hostile congressional attitude, not to foreign policy considerations. Even during the cold war years and the increasingly enormous military budget, it is unlikely that had that money not been spent on the armed services it would have been spent on social services; most of it would probably have stayed in the taxpayers' pockets. It is precisely because of this negative congressional behavior that liberals since the 1930s have regarded a powerful president as the best hope of achieving a just society that helps its needy and underprivileged. Nevertheless, the post-1945 emergence of Russia as the dominant Eurasian power, while the states of Western Europe collapsed, did mean that presidents became absorbed with the task of avoiding a nuclear conflagration in a bipolar world of frequent confrontations and crises while simultaneously defending American interests. Thus the great demands on the time and energies of the country's political and intellectual leaders and on its economic resources reinforced the neglect of domestic problems.

THE ABILITY TO ACT: INFORMATION AS A POLITICAL RESOURCE

If by background, personal inclination, and political necessity the president is likely to put foreign policy ahead of domestic concerns, it is also true that he has the resources needed to be preeminent in this area of policy-making. One of the president's advantages over Congress in foreign policy is the vast amounts of information he has at his fingertips. "Power is knowledge," and the foreign policy bureaucracy possesses such knowledge. The president can call upon the State and

Defense Departments, the Central Intelligence Agency, the Arms Control and Disarmament Agency, the U.S. Information Agency (propaganda), the Agency for International Development (economic aid), and the foreign staffs in such other departments as Commerce, Treasury, and Agriculture. All these agencies are represented in the embassies abroad and participate in the making of foreign policy in Washington; abroad, they are also amply represented outside the embassies, often by delegations of at least equal size to that of the State Department's foreign service.

To gain some sense of the size of the president's foreign policy bureaucracy, we need but look at the size of the State Department—the *smallest* of the three senior foreign policy agencies—when the Nixon Administration came into office in 1969. It had a budget of $400 million and a staff of 12,000 (7,000 in the United States, 5,000 abroad); by contrast, the Defense Department had a budget of almost $78 billion, 1.2 million civilian employees, and 3.3 million in the armed forces.[3] Figures on the CIA are unknown, but its budget and personnel figures are far greater than those of the State Department.

A sense of the growth of the State Department's staff since just before World War II, as the country emerged from its isolationist shell, is apparent in Table 2-2. While the secretary of state's staff had grown to 342 by 1969, the Joint Chiefs of Staff in the Defense Department alone has a Joint Staff of 400, and in actuality the total figure comes to nearly double that number.[4]

It is not surprising that in these circumstances Congress should be dependent upon the executive for its information. This is particularly true when compared to domestic affairs. Here, a representative or senator can call upon the appropriate executive departments dealing with the problem and numerous interest groups, as well as rely upon his own familiarity with the problems being considered by the committee (e.g., congressmen from agricultural areas may serve on the agriculture committee). He has, in brief, means not only to check out what "the facts" really are but also experience from which to gain his own sense of perspective on executive policy recommendations. But on foreign policy issues Congress must rely

TABLE 2–2.   Staffing the Department of State

Category	1938	1948	1969
Secretary's Office (including secretariat and under secretaries)	21	186	342
Geographic political offices*	112	318	980
Functional offices Economic, Intelligence, U.N., Educational, Scientific, Legal, Protocol, etc.	387	881	1,645
Administrative offices (including consular divisions)	443	2,813	3,307
Miscellaneous (personnel seconded to other agencies, in training, on leave status)	—	—	600
Totals	963	4,198	6,874

* African Affairs, Inter-American Affairs, East Asian and Pacific Affairs, European Affairs, Near Eastern and South Asian Affairs.
SOURCE: Table 2 of *The Foreign Affairs Fudge Factory,* by John Campbell, © 1971 by Basic Books, Inc., Publishers, New York.

primarily upon information supplied by the president and the foreign policy bureaucracy. And given the facts of life for most congressmen—that they must devote a lot of time to their constituents' affairs; they are members of one or more committees in which most of Congress's work is accomplished; and they themselves feel that they have far less competency and knowledge of external than of internal problems—this reliance is understandable.

This reliance is, in fact, twofold. First, it applies to the "facts" which most congressmen do not even have the time to digest. Thus, when Congress was deciding on the Marshall Plan for the reconstruction of postwar Europe, a highly imaginative policy that signaled a revolutionary shift of American policy from its prewar isolationism to a postwar commitment to Europe—a course Congress had rejected in 1919—this exchange occurred between the Staff Director of the Republican Policy Committee and Republican Senator Homer Ferguson (Mich.):

MR. SMITH: Now, Senators, for your amusement as well as to bear out my point on the impossible work load put upon members of Congress, I have gathered here a group of the books and reports, limited solely to an official character, which you should be reading now on the Marshall Plan.

[MR. SMITH here presented a stack of material 18 inches high.]

You are going to take the momentous step in the history of this country when you pass upon the Marshall plan. . . . That is what you ought to be studying. It contains the Krug report, the Harriman report, the State Department report, the reports of the Herter committee, the Foreign Relations Committee digest; it includes part of the hearings just completed of the Foreign Relations Committee. It does not include hearings yet to be held by the Appropriations Committees. This is one work load you have now on a single problem out of the many problems you have to decide.

SENATOR FERGUSON: How long would it take in your opinion . . . for a person to read it?

MR. SMITH. Well, Senator, I have been reading for the last 35 years, nearly all my life, in the field of research; and if I could do an intelligent job on that in 2 months of solid reading excluding myself from everything else . . . I would credit myself with great efficiency.

SENATOR FERGUSON: A normal person would probably take 4 to 5 months.[5]

How in these circumstances can a legislator become familiar with such intricate problems as arms control negotiations, the nature of nationalism in some Third World region, the complexities of Sino-Soviet relations, the intentions of both Russia and China toward the major non-Communist states, or the strategic doctrine, force levels, and arms composition of the U.S. military? These and the multiple other issues confronting Congress are issues on which even the experts may not have all the facts and on which, even with sufficient facts, they would disagree as to meaning, consequences, and what ought to be done.

Of course, all of this assumes that Congress gets the information. After it was disclosed in 1973 that the United States had been secretly bombing Cambodia during 1969–70, a number of senators were critical of Secretary of State Rogers for not discussing this issue with them fully at the time. A State Department spokesman said in reply that Rogers had mentioned the raids on two occasions while testifying before the Foreign Relations Committee, although he admitted the secretary had not volunteered information on the magnitude of the raids. He added that if Rogers had been asked for details of the bombing, the secretary would have provided any requested information! But how were senators to ask questions about a military operation of which they were unaware and about which they had learned only a few details from the *New York Times?* The utter dependence of senators on the executive for information could not be more clearly illustrated than by this admittedly exceptional example. If the executive withholds information, Congress may remain in ignorance.

But Congress is dependent upon the executive not only for "the facts" but for their interpretation as well. For example, in 1947 the Truman Administration had to reach a decision about intervening in the Eastern Mediterranean, where the Russians were putting great pressure on Turkey for control of the Dardanelles and on Greece, where a civil war involving the Greek Communists was raging. There was little precedent for American involvement in that area of the world. While Congress had become increasingly anti-Russian during spats with Moscow in 1946, it was also in a fierce budget-cutting mood and averse to vast, expensive external commitments in January, 1947. Thus when in February the British informed the State Department that they could no longer support both endangered countries, the Truman Administration decided that American power had to contain what it perceived to be Russian expansion. As the states of Europe collapsed, symbolized by Britain's collapse, the postwar bipolar balance emerged.

On the Eurasian continent, Russia was emerging as the dominant state; only the United States, separated from Eurasia by the Atlantic and Pacific Oceans, could supply the countervailing power. President Truman called together a congressional delegation to declare his intentions, but it initially reacted skeptically and interpreted Truman's proposed action as pulling British chestnuts out of the fire. Secretary of State Marshall and Under Secretary Acheson contested this interpretation, and Acheson particularly stressed American security considerations. Convinced, the congressmen insisted Truman explain his dramatic reversal of traditional American policy before Congress and the nation. In an address to a joint session of both houses, Truman informed Congress of the situations in Turkey and Greece and then outlined the basis of the new containment policy. He disguised the basic power realities motivating U.S. actions, however, and justified them on ideological grounds.[6]

Perhaps another example is pertinent since Congress, especially the senate, in the late 1960s turned critical of the American involvement in Vietnam. Johnson inherited a situation in which only ad hoc decisions had been made in response to immediate problems; the Kennedy Administration, Arthur Schlesinger, Jr., has suggested, was occupied with other more urgent issues, such as the abortive Cuban invasion, the Berlin Wall, crises in Laos and the Congo, the Alliance for Progress, and the Limited Nuclear Test Ban.[7] Only piecemeal economic and military commitments had been made; each constituted the minimally necessary step to prevent a Communist victory. At no point were the fundamental questions and long-range implications of an increasing Vietnam involvement analyzed: Was South Vietnam vital to American security? Would its fall represent the consolidation of one country under a nationalist leader or constitute a "falling domino" in the Communization of all of Southeast Asia? Did the political situation in South Vietnam warrant or preclude American intervention? Were political conditions both in the United States and in South Vietnam conducive to effective military action? How large a commitment would the United States be required to make, and what costs should be expected? What role should Saigon and its forces play?

If these questions were even asked by President Kennedy and his advisers, the answers did not provide guidelines for the policies that were ultimately followed. The assumption was that South Vietnam was vital, a test of the credibility of America's commitments and power. Policy was built upon that assumption. The approach was incremental and, as the overall situation deteriorated badly, Johnson, like Kennedy, continued to react to the symptoms of the problem and applied short-range solutions: first covert operations, then increasingly frequent "retaliatory" air strikes against North Vietnam, followed by around-the-clock bombing and, finally, the use of U.S. ground forces in South Vietnam.

What is noticeable in retrospect is not only the administration's lack of questions but also Congress's. Congressmen may not always know the facts or be sufficiently expert in foreign policy, but their expertise is supposed to be something more fundamental, a political judgment as to the viability of policy, an ability to question the experts' views based upon specialized knowledge. But neither the Senate nor any of its committees, including Foreign Relations and Armed Services, raised any of the fundamental questions that should have been answered before the 1965 intervention. As before, the Senate and House followed the executive's lead; their criticism came after the intervention, and then only after the intervention went sour.

Yet, ironically, while unassertive on the Indochina issue, Congress's intensely emotional response to the collapse of Nationalist China played a key role in the Vietnamese intervention. The congressional Republicans' attempt to blame the "loss of China" on Truman, their condemnation of alleged Democratic "softness" on communism, and their charges of treason compelled the Democrats to pursue a vigorous anti-Communist course in Asia to avoid a recurrence of such charges. Neither Kennedy nor Johnson wanted to be accused of the "loss of Indochina." Thus it was not congressional questioning of the anti-Communist assumptions that motivated the Kennedy and Johnson administrations but the anticipation that the Congress would blame them for not being anti-Communist enough that greatly reinforced the two presidents' inclination to prevent North Vietnam, the perceived aggressor in South Vietnam, from taking over the non-Communist half of that country. Congressional reassertion, frequently looked to in the post-Vietnam era as a restraint upon allegedly bellicose presidents, may on occasion therefore have quite the opposite results.

In any event, it is unlikely that the information and interpretation "gap" between the executive and legislative branches will soon disappear. It may, to be sure, be narrowed as the appropriate congressional committees obtain larger and better staffs to develop their own sources of information and policy advice, take more investigative trips abroad, and are more critical in cross-examining administration witnesses. And the Vietnam War may well lead the Congress, particularly the Senate, to concern itself more with the assumptions underlying specific policies and the likely consequences of their adoption. Still, the resources of the executive remain overwhelming by comparison, and it will not be much easier in the future than in the past to change policies that an administration insists are of vital importance to the national interest.

This is particularly true since the increasing centralization and institutionalization of foreign policy in the White House have raised the question of the status of the president's assistant on national security policy. If, as during the first five years of the Nixon Administration, the secretary of state is not the primary foreign policy adviser to the president—if, indeed, he seems not to be involved in formulating basic policies—cross-examining the secretary in congressional hearings is not of much value to the Congress. The president's national security assistant is a personal adviser and has a privileged relationship with his chief; he is responsible only to him, not to Congress. But unless he testifies before the relevant committees, how will the Congress receive its information and ask the necessary critical questions about policy? It will be interesting to follow Kissinger's combination of the dual roles.

THE WILLINGNESS TO ACT: WIELDING THE SWORD

Besides the advantage of knowledge, the president possesses the further advantage of being able to act. It is, of course, this capacity to initiate action—especially the commitment of U.S. forces, when the President deems it necessary—that has been greatly responsible for the expansion of presidential power in foreign policy since the Nazi and Japanese threats of the late 1930s; and it is this capacity that is at the heart of the contemporary controversy over the extent of presidential powers. Not that this expansion started in the 1930s. For example, the Constitution stated that the president could receive and send ambassadors. President Washington interpreted this as conferring upon the presidency the power of diplomatic recognition by receiving Citizen Genêt of the French Republic. Congress, of course, has on occasion exerted its influence on this issue, as it did after 1949, when it consistently warned successive presidents not to extend recognition to Communist China. Still, a determined President Nixon, with his surprise 1971 announcement that he would visit Peking, quickly turned the tables on the opponents of recognizing Communist China and showed once again that it is largely the president who determines the question of recognizing foreign governments. By seizing the initiative, he left the congressional opponents no time to organize. The president's subsequent steps—his visits with Mao Tse-tung and Chou En-lai and the 1973 opening of Chinese and American "liaison missions" in Washington and Peking, respectively—established formal diplomatic relations in all but name; the removal of this "disguise" was only a matter of time. The president's actions were "positive"; Congress's power, in this case used to oppose recognition, was negative.

Presidents not only exploited the "great silences" of the Constitution to "make foreign policy" and enhance the powers of their office, but also used them to seize the initiative and strengthen their position against Congress. In this connection, presidents have long resorted to setting policy in declarations or by their behavior. A Monroe announces his Doctrine or a Truman declares, as he did in early 1947, that "it must be the policy of the United States to support free peoples who are resisting attempted subjugation by armed minorities or outside pressure." Or a president may visit West Berlin, as Kennedy did, thus reinforcing in the minds of his NATO allies and Soviet adversary the American commitment to that city and Western Europe; he may visit the capital of a nation not previously recognized, as Nixon did on his trip to Peking, signaling a radical shift of policy; and he may welcome a foreign leader to Washington, as Nixon again did with Brezhnev, the Soviet Communist party leader, thereby indicating a certain atmosphere and expectations about future American-Soviet relations that would have been somewhat different had the meeting occurred in Iceland or Switzerland. Or he can express his "concern" and "lack of satisfaction" with specific policies toward certain nations, as Nixon frequently did after the Vietnamese cease-fire agreements of January, 1973, implying or expressing remedial courses the United States might adopt. (Such was later discovered in a letter Nixon wrote to South Vietnamese President Thieu in order to encourage him to sign the peace agreement. In it the president promised to react with force—presumably, air power—if the North Vietnamese violated the accord.) Similarly, a president can express sentiments of support for a particular state so often, as a series of American presidents have in fact done with regard to Israel, that a virtual commitment of defense seems to exist even though no treaty to this effect has ever been approved by the Senate. Indeed, former Senator Fulbright used to suggest that the United States sign a treaty in order to *delimit* our unspoken commitment.

The point of these examples is threefold: one, the president, by what he says and does—and, on occasion, by *not* saying or *not* doing—sets the direction and tone of U. S. foreign policy; two, by exercising his initiative the president leaves Congress with little option but to follow him, unless it wishes publicly to humiliate him and undermine his position as the nation's spokesman in international affairs; and three, the president has an array of tools—informal, such as the ones just discussed, as well as more formal ones—at his disposal, which enable him to use his advantages.

One of the more formal tools the president can use to draw public attention to certain issues and his suggested solutions is the draft treaty. Although the Senate may be consulted during the drafting and negotiating of a treaty and may give consent when it is submitted, the end of the negotiating process with the other country involved really commits the United States, unless the Senate wants to erode other nations' confidence in the president's ability to represent and articulate American interests internationally. Ever since defeat of the Versailles Peace Treaty concluding World War I, the Senate has been reluctant to deny ratification. For example, when a president is negotiating a limitation of strategic arms, the publicity alone by the time the treaty reaches the Senate floor makes the draft difficult to defeat. Arms control measures are probably particularly so. If an administration has initialed a draft treaty that has the support—or at least the acquiescence—of the various interested executive agencies involved, such as the Joint Chiefs of Staff, it can "sell" such measures to Congress and the public, because arms control often takes on the appearance of a combination of motherhood and salvation and can be easily identified with that most cherished of values, peace. When such a measure is signed in Moscow by the president himself, as Nixon did with the Strategic Arms Limitations Treaty (SALT I) and this is fully covered by television (as were the president's return to the United States and his immediate journey to Capitol Hill to report the success of his negotiations in building a more stable "structure of peace"), who can really do more than raise some objections and then approve such a clearly worthy enterprise when the president has already gone over Congress's head to the country?

But this is also true of a treaty of defense against Moscow, as the signing of the NATO treaty in 1949, which can be identified with another highly regarded value, national security. In these two cases, SALT I and NATO, Nixon did not solicit the Senate's advice, but Truman did. In both, however, the Senate gave its consent. Not that this is automatic. There may be long hearings in which the opponents to the treaty, both within the government and outside, will be heard; some senators may be critical and wary, and the administration may have to reassure the Senate that no hidden commitments or dangers to the country are involved. But the president is not repudiated or sent back to the negotiating table to negotiate further changes.

Although some of the most fundamental U.S. policies since 1945 have been submitted to the Senate in order to let the American people know what commitments their government has undertaken on their behalf and to signal to the adversary the nature of American interests, treaties are few and far between. Presidents often bypass the Senate, with its demand for a two-thirds majority approval of treaties, by resorting to executive agreements, which do not need legislative approval. (Executive agreements may, of course, also be negotiated and signed in pursuance of a particular objective authorized by Congress, e.g., specific tariff agreements with individual countries after Congress has approved a general tariff bill.) Indeed, executive agreements outnumber treaties, although, like treaties, they may commit the United States to the defense of other countries or involve it in situations that may involve the use of force. Thus, for example, a series of executive agreements with Spain for American military bases since 1953 are virtually tantamount to a military commitment to Spain, even though the Senate in 1970 adopted a non-binding resolution expressing the view that the 1970 executive agreement signed by Spain and the Nixon administration should not be construed as a U.S. commitment to the defense of Spain. In 1976, an agreement for the continued use of American bases in Spain was finally put in treaty form, giving the United States the opportunity to deny the existence of a defense commitment to Spain. (Of course, whether such a commitment does not in fact exist once American forces in Spain are attacked, regardless of a Senate resolution or treaty denying such an obligation, is another question.) The trend toward executive agreements on important issues is demonstrated by two other Nixon agreements: The Paris peace agreement ending the Vietnam War (at least, officially) and the five-year freeze on offensive arms negotiated as part of the SALT I package were both executive agreements (although the ABM limitation was incorporated in a treaty, as is likely to happen with a SALT II offensive weapons agreement, if one is reached).

No executive agreement is ever likely to be more dramatic than Franklin Roosevelt's Destroyer Deal of 1940. England, all alone against Nazi Germany after the fall of France, desperately needed destroyers to help guard the English Channel against a threatened German invasion and help convoys of supplies from America across the Atlantic Ocean. Confronted by a Congress in which isolationist attitudes were strongly represented, the president made a deal he could present to the public as aiding hemispheric defense: an exchange of fifty World War I-vintage destroyers for a lease of naval bases on Caribbean islands controlled by Britain. The deal, embodied in an executive agreement, symbolized a significant first step in an increasingly perceptible commitment to Britain's defense, indeed, its survival, which was to occur throughout 1941 in the period before Pearl Harbor.

But it is the president's authority as commander-in-chief that has become the greatest source of his expanded power in this century. In 1900 President McKinley sent troops to China to join an international army to crush the Boxer Rebellion, which had besieged foreign embassies in Peking. Theodore Roosevelt, Wilson, and Coolidge used the marines at will throughout the Caribbean. Woodrow Wilson sent troops into Mexico to pursue Pancho Villa and had Vera Cruz bombarded before the outbreak of World War I. In early 1917, when the Germans declared unrestricted submarine warfare on all shipping, belligerent and neutral, to starve Britain into submission, Wilson armed American merchantmen taking supplies to England. Wilson acted after the Senate refused to sanction the president's request for authorizing armaments for the self-defense of the ships. When, during the later Russian Civil War, the Japanese sought to exploit that conflict and establish themselves in Siberia by landing troops, Wilson sent American troops to keep an eye on the Japanese. After the eruption of World War II and the fall of France, and after both the Destroyer Deal and congressional approval of the Lend-Lease aid program, the problem was how to get the munitions to England, since the Royal Navy was still strung too thin. In the fall of 1941, Roosevelt began to use American warships to escort the English and Canadian merchantmen that had joined American ships in taking supplies to U.S. forces in Iceland, where the British Royal Navy took over; he also ordered American ships to "shoot on sight" if they came across German raiders or submarines.

Since World War II, recurrent crises—with the potential of exploding into nuclear war—as well as two limited wars have built on these precedents and further expanded the president's authority as commander-in-chief. When the Russians blockaded Berlin in 1948, President Truman responded with an airlift to supply the population of the Western half of the city. When the North Koreans attacked South Korea in 1950, the president ordered first air support for the South Korean Army and then the landing of American ground forces in Korea when the air support seemed unable to stem the invaders. Congressional leaders were informed of these decisions by the president, but he did not ask for their approval. Truman felt that as commander-in-chief he already possessed the authority to commit U.S. forces when he believed American security was endangered. After Communist China's intervention in Korea, he sent several divisions to Western Europe to enhance Western strength and deter a possible Russian move in Moscow's "front yard" while America was becoming more deeply involved in Asia; again Congress was not asked for approval. Both Eisenhower and Kennedy made commitments to South Vietnam. The former initiated a large-scale program of economic and military assistance to support the non-Communist government there. "The United States had gradually developed a special commitment in South Vietnam. It was certainly not absolutely binding—but the commitment was there."[8] Kennedy would enlarge this into what the Pentagon Papers refer to as a "broad commitment"[9] and would leave his successor feeling that this commitment was virtually binding.

The Kennedy involvement was piecemeal: By the time of the president's assassination, 16,500 military "advisers" were in South Vietnam, a symptom and symbol of the increasing American political commitment to the survival of a non-Communist southern half of Vietnam. Kennedy's alleged involvement in the overthrow and unintended assassination of President Diem was, after all, based upon the expectation that a new military government would more effectively wage the war against the Vietcong. Kennedy also launched the abortive invasion of Cuba in 1961 and blockaded the island a year later to compel the Soviets to withdraw their missiles. And Johnson intervened in the Dominican Republic in 1965 with troops to forestall "another Cuba" (Eisenhower had earlier, in 1954, covertly used the CIA, rather than the marines, to overthrow the government of Guatemala when it was feared to be moving in Moscow's direction).

It was, however, the increasing unpopularity of America's first modern limited war, the Korean War, that led President Eisenhower after the Democrats had been defeated in 1952 to ask for congressional resolutions granting him legislative support to use the armed forces when he felt this to be necessary in the national interest. The administration's idea was that "the resolution process, by involving Congress in the take-off, would incriminate it in a crash-landing."[10] In other words, a principal purpose was to ward off the type of later congressional criticism and retribution that had hurt the Truman Administration. The resolution was not requested because Eisenhower, any more than his predecessors or successors, felt that in the absence of congressional support he did not possess the legal authority to use the armed forces as he saw fit—as, for example, in Lebanon or the Formosa Straits. In any event, Congress gave him virtually a blank check; in fact, it was more an expression of approval than a grant of authority.

Johnson, in 1964, received a similar broad grant known as the Tonkin resolution after the gulf where North Vietnamese torpedo boats allegedly attacked two American destroyers. This is how in part it was worded:

> [Be it] Resolved by the Senate and House of Representatives of the United States of America in Congress assembled, That the Congress approves and supports the determination of the President, as Commander in Chief, to take all necessary measures to repel any armed attack against the forces of the United States and to prevent further aggression.
>
> The United States regards as vital to its national interest and to world peace the maintenance of international peace and security in Southeast Asia. Consonant with the Constitution and the Charter of the United Nations and in accordance with its obligations under the Southeast Asia Collective Defense Treaty, the United States is, therefore, prepared, as the President determines, to take all necessary steps, including the use of armed force, to assist any member or protocol state of the Southeast Asia Collective Defense Treaty requesting assistance in defense of its freedom.[11]

Johnson, unfortunately for the nation as well as himself, was neither lucky nor shrewd.[12] Both he and Eisenhower requested congressional resolutions for the areas in which action was contemplated when tensions there appeared to be quite high. In each case Congress, once the president had publicly requested its support, could hardly turn him down unless it wished to seem unpatriotic. Eisenhower, however, was either lucky or shrewd. In neither crisis was he required to use force overtly. In the Middle East, troops landed in Lebanon but were not involved in any fighting, and in the Formosa Straits the Seventh Fleet "showed the flag" but did not need to shoot.

Johnson had hoped that the Tonkin resolution, passed by the Senate with only two dissenting votes and by the House unanimously, would be read by Hanoi as an indication of American determination to prevent a Communist takeover of South Vietnam and the virtually unanimous congressional and public support the president had for this purpose. But neither the resolution nor some retaliatory strikes after Tonkin and, later, Pleiku led Hanoi to "leave its neighbor alone," as Secretary of State Rusk phrased the American objective. More punishing moves, it was felt, were needed to attain this aim. Sustained air attacks that avoided city bombing were launched in the spring of 1965; when those also did not frighten off Hanoi, presumed to be the organizer and director of the war in the South, Johnson felt he had no choice but to send American troops into South Vietnam as the military situation there deteriorated rapidly and the Vietcong appeared to be within reach of victory. But as the increasingly Americanized war dragged on and victory seemed more and more to be an illusion, congressional and public support for the war declined, as it had earlier for the war in Korea. As the criticism mounted, Johnson was not protected by the Tonkin resolution. The conclusion would, therefore, seem to be that congressional support in the form of a resolution for presidential use of force is politically largely immaterial. If a president is successful he will receive little or no criticism—indeed much praise—even without a congressional resolution; if he is unsuccessful, he will reap large amounts of criticism and abuse, even if he possesses hundreds of congressional resolutions.

In any event, once the country is involved in a war, whether it is legally declared by the Congress or not, presidents make the basic political decisions and choose the appropriate military strategy to achieve the chosen political objectives. Thus, Roosevelt during World War II decided that Germany should be defeated before Japan since Germany was the stronger power and the United States, as a belligerent, had allies whose existence was threatened primarily by Germany, not Japan. Later, Roosevelt chose to invade continental Europe through France rather than, as Churchill wanted, to drive into the Balkans from northern Italy and Yugoslavia, thereby trying to limit the Red Army's advance and Soviet influence to Eastern Europe. A cross-channel invasion, which would come to grips with the German Army on the plains of Europe where it could

be defeated, seemed to Roosevelt a more feasible way to end
the war quickly; it undoubtedly was, but it did mean that the
Red Army stood in the heart of Europe after Germany's collapse.

During the Korean War President Truman, who had already
made the key decisions to drop two atomic bombs to force
Japan's surrender and to intervene in Korea, made two further
significant decisions: one, to cross the 38th Parallel dividing
North and South Korea after the North Korean Army had been
defeated; and two, not to extend the war even farther by
bombing and blockading China after the Chinese had responded to the U.S. invasion of North Korea by intervening,
just as the North Korean invasion of the South has precipitated
American intervention. This brought Truman into a fierce
confrontation with the commanding general, General MacArthur, a great war hero, who was supported by the conservative
and dominant wing of the Republican party in Congress.
When MacArthur refused to stop publicly criticizing the administration's policy and strategy in Korea with the assertion
that there was "no substitute for victory," Truman fired him
amid a public furor.[13]

For Johnson, of course, all the decisions in Vietnam proved
fateful: the decision in 1965 to escalate the American intervention with air power and troops until U.S. forces in Vietnam
stood at over 500,000 men; further decisions to escalate in
order to appease congressional hawks and de-escalate to satisfy
the doves; and the decision to fight a "painless war" until 1967
by deferring students and postponing a war tax to counter the
rising inflation, among other measures. But as the intervention
turned sour, it stained Johnson's historical reputation, precipitated an executive-legislative struggle, badly divided the nation, compelled Johnson to foreswear renomination as the
Democrat's presidential candidate in 1968, deeply divided the
Democratic party, and helped the Republicans win the presidency that year.

After President Nixon had come into office, the Senate repealed the Tonkin resolution not once but twice! Nixon even
supported this move, claiming that he did not need it, and
thereby added insult to the injury the Senate already felt at
what it claimed was Johnson's deception at the time he re-

quested the Tonkin resolution. Although it had given him a broad grant of authority, senatorial critics now asserted, it had done so on the assumption that Johnson would use it only for his retaliatory strikes, *not* to justify the widening of the war with large-scale American intervention.[14] But Nixon, whose policy was to withdraw U.S. ground forces gradually while letting the South Vietnamese Army increasingly take over the fighting as its capability to do so was presumably enhanced by better training and more weapons, claimed that as commander-in-chief he had the authority to use the armed forces in any way he wished to protect the remaining American forces in Vietnam.

As more troops were pulled out and Hanoi's temptation to attack in South Vietnam increased, Nixon undertook a number of actions—vigorously criticized in the Senate—under the commander-in-chief authority he had claimed. He ordered American forces into Cambodia to search for and destroy North Vietnamese supplies. (Before this action in 1970, as noted earlier, U.S. bombers had long carried on bombing attacks in Cambodia, which were hidden from congressional and public scrutiny.) Nixon also sent American planes from time to time for "protective reaction" raids on the North; authorized the mining of North Vietnamese ports and heavy bombing of Hanoi and Haiphong after Hanoi launched a large conventional attack on South Vietnam; and, when the Paris peace negotiations stalled, launched B-52s during the Christmas season to compel a settlement (in January, 1973, a settlement was signed). After the Paris peace agreement, when the understanding that a cease-fire and withdrawal of U.S. forces from South Vietnam would be followed shortly by cease-fires in Laos and Cambodia failed to materialize in Cambodia, B-52s were used to stem the successful Communist forces. Since the president could no longer invoke his need to protect American troops after they had departed, he claimed that the failure of the Communists to abide by the Paris agreement meant that he could wage the war in Cambodia until a cease-fire had been agreed upon. He had possessed the authority to wage the war in Vietnam; this authority continued until the war in Cambodia ended as it had in South Vietnam. The Congress disagreed and cut off funds for further bombing in 1973.

In an attempt to terminate the bombing even before the cut-off date, a suit was brought in federal court on the basis that Congress had not declared a war in Cambodia and that consequently the president's action was unconstitutional. The suit was eventually unsuccessful, but at some point it is likely that the Supreme Court will have to rule on the whole issue of the president's war power. In the past, the Court has generally been reluctant to challenge the president's exercise of his power, even when he has exercised it in unprecedented ways. Whether it can or will continue this general abstention on the crucial, central issue of the force remains to be seen.

In any event, it is perhaps ironic that while the Constitution confers upon Congress the power to declare war and the president the power to conduct war, Vietnam more than any other post-World War II crisis demonstrated that, while presidents increasingly resort to force without a congressional declaration of war, Congress increasingly wants a say in the conduct of the conflict. What is clear is that in a world of neither total war nor harmonious peace, a world in which it is no longer fashionable to declare war, but which remains nevertheless unhappily too frequently a world of crises, limited war, and international tension, the "way we go to war" and the manner in which we fight wars have changed.

The principal means of dealing with this problem and restoring Congress's role in decisions involving the use of force, has been the War Powers Act which passed the Senate and House over President Nixon's veto in 1973. The bill provides for three emergency situations in which the president can commit American forces without prior congressional declaration of war: to repel or forestall an attack upon the United States; to repel or forestall an attack upon American forces located outside the country; to rescue endangered American citizens in carefully defined circumstances; beyond these emergency categories, the president would need "specific statutory authorization."[15] This requirement aims to replace the blank-check resolution such as the Gulf of Tonkin with precisely worded resolutions, jointly devised by Congress and the president. Even when the president uses his emergency powers, he must immediately make a full report to Congress and obtain congressional authority to continue the action after sixty days, with an extension of thirty additional days if troops are in danger. If he fails to receive legislative concurrence, he must terminate the action at that time. Even before this sixty-day deadline Congress can terminate the action through a concurrent resolution, which would not be subject to a presidential veto. As one of the bill's sponsors said, "The real danger is that presidents can—and do—shoot from the hip. If the collective judgment of the president and Congress is required to go to war, it will call for responsible action by the Congress for which each member must answer individually and for restraint by both the Congress and the presidents."[16] The War Powers Act, in short, grants the Congress the potential to play a greater role in decisions involving the use of force.

In reality, however, not much has yet changed. The act, in a sense, recognized "reality," for it changed the Constitution from reading that war cannot be waged without the consent of Congress to the president can wage war until Congress stops him. When the U.S. merchant ship *Mayaguez* was seized in what the American government claimed to be the high seas by the Cambodians shortly after the final collapse of South Vietnam in 1975, the president used American military forces to recover the ship and its crew on the island where they were and, to prevent any retaliation, ordered some bombing of certain airfields and port targets on the mainland. President Ford did inform the Congress, as the War Powers Act required, of what had occurred and what he was going to do about it. But he no more consulted Congress than had his predecessors. The ship and crew were recovered, although not without loss of life, and the action was generally applauded as successful and having saved a tattered American prestige, which had been badly deflated by the demise of South Vietnam and was widely judged as further deflated by Cambodia's action. Therefore, a mini-power as Cambodia could not be permitted to seize and hold a U.S. ship with impunity without lowering American self-esteem—and, perhaps, prestige as seen in Moscow and elsewhere. Ford had rescued this prestige and, as a result, his popularity in the country rose to his highest yet. Thus, instead of being criticized by the Congress he had essentially bypassed, he was praised by Republicans and Democrats alike. To repeat: If a president is unsuccessful when he uses force, he will be damned even if he has legislative support; if successful, he will be acclaimed even if he does not possess congressional support. Perhaps the real test of the War Powers Act will come when the president confronts a situation involving a more sustained and far bigger military involvement than the rescue of the *Mayaguez* needed.

3

THE DECISION-MAKING ARENA: THE CAST OF CHARACTERS

THE CIRCLES OF POWER: AN OVERVIEW

Because the stakes in foreign policy decision-making are generally seen as quite different from those in domestic policies, it is not surprising to find that some of the major actors on domestic policy such as the Congress, political parties, interest groups, and public opinion play a lesser role in foreign policy decision-making. It is the presidency which is well suited as an office for handling questions that have high stakes and may require quick and decisive action.

The decision-making arena on foreign policy questions is best described as a set of concentric circles.[1] (See Figure 3-1.) The smallest, inner circle contains the actors who actually make the decisions on most foreign policy questions. Here we find the president and his closest advisers. Beyond this inner circle are three further circles. Each has successively less impact on foreign policy decisions. The second circle is composed of bureaucracies in the major foreign policy agencies and the armed services, the second-rank and less influential foreign policy departments, presidential advisers and cabinet members whose primary responsibility is in the domestic sphere but who may be consulted on foreign policy questions, and scientists. In the third circle we find Congress, political parties, and interest groups; and in the fourth, outer circle are public opinion and the media.

Figure 3–1. The Concentric Circles of Power in Foreign
Policy Decision-Making

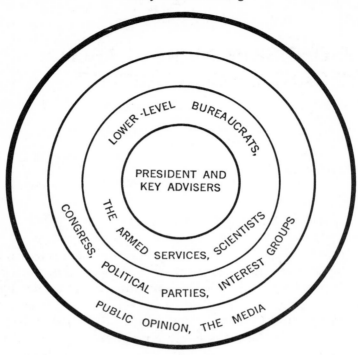

On domestic policy, lines of authority cut across the national, state, and local levels and across the executive, legislative, and judicial branches as well. In contrast, the arena of foreign policy decision-making is exclusively at the national level, is concentrated in the executive branch, and is therefore clearly hierarchical. Still, it would be misleading to distinguish in this regard between all of domestic policy on the one hand and all of foreign policy on the other. Increasingly, foreign policy decisions have domestic repercussions, for example, food and energy policies, as well as the more traditional "mixed" issues such as the defense budget and trade legislation. Every dollar spent on defense is a dollar that cannot be spent on domestic programs. Wheat exported to the Soviet Union is unavailable for the domestic market, and, thus, the cost to the American consumer increases. The government of Saudi Arabia has directly stated that it expects a moderation in the American position on the Middle East conflict in return for the Saudis'

decision to hold down the price of oil. In the case of trade, foreign policy decisions give some groups cause to perceive themselves as "winners" and other as "losers," and in those areas the president is no longer dominant. Rather, the various actors who play an important role in domestic legislation will have a greater impact on these foreign-domestic policies than on crisis decisions.

In crisis decision-making, the three outer circles play at best an advisory or supportive role in policy formation. The greater the domestic repercussions there are on a foreign policy decision, the greater the role of each outer circle in the actual decision-making process. Again, the question is one of *how* the stakes are perceived, even on those "intermestic" policies which have both foreign and domestic repercussions. The Soviet wheat deal in 1973 did not arouse much controversy in the two outer circles until the domestic winners (producers) and losers (smaller farmers and consumers) were clearly identified. On energy issues, the dominant theme is still one of "we–they," so that the oil-exporting nations comprising OPEC rather than the big oil companies (predominantly American-owned) are seen as the "villains." The distinction between crisis situations and those foreign policy issues which resemble domestic policies is not simply a question of determining the extent to which there are few or many actors in a particular context. Rather, the question of stakes is more complex. On the one hand, as we shall see below, crisis decision-making in foreign policy is quite different from domestic policy formation. Yet, the issues which involve both foreign and domestic politics are not all of one kind. There are the more traditionally "mixed" domestic-foreign issues such as trade and the defense budget, on the one hand. On the other hand, we note the increasing number of policies which were long perceived as predominantly domestic (e.g., energy and food), but have now become "intermestic." On these latter issues, the basic conflicts will resemble the most traditional domestic policies. Decisions will not be based upon foreign policy considerations, although the international arena will affect the policy alternatives and even the process of reaching decisions. The stakes will be perceived in terms of domestic group conflict in that legislators and bureaucrats will select the alternatives which resolve group conflict. However, the scope of these alternatives may now be affected (limited) by actors outside the United States. For example, energy policy can no longer be considered in isolation of the production quotas and price levels set by oil-producing nations—even if those nations are not part of the group conflict in the United States which leads to a policy choice.

The example of limited wars, such as the Korean and Vietnam conflicts, also demonstrates the point that the more domestic repercussions a foreign policy issue has, the greater the role of each outer circle in the actual decision-making. Support for each was quite high at the beginning of the American involvement. Public opinion, congressional attitudes, and the sentiments of actors in the two innermost circles all were supportive of the president's policies. Indeed, very little was heard from either Congress or the public. However, as the wars dragged on with no end in sight, the stakes involved began to change in the perceptions of many actors. Key members of Congress attacked American involvement in each war, public opinion polls gradually showed a shift against the president's policies in each case, and the third and fourth circles became relevant actors in the policy-making process. The longer a foreign policy issue remains unresolved, the more likely the public's perceptions of the costs will change. In the case of total wars, such as World War II, popular support does not necessarily decline as the war effort is carried out over time.[2] However, in limited wars, the stakes have never been as clear as they are in "total" wars. Thus, the type of decision is not the only consideration to determine how many actors will be involved in the decision-making process. How long the decision takes to be make and the stakes involved are also key factors, as are the president's own inclinations about which actors he wants to bring into the arena. In the rest of this chapter, we shall examine the roles played by the various actors in each of our four circles.

THE INNER CIRCLE: PRESIDENTIAL DOMINANCE

At the center of the inner circle, of course, stands the president. In addition, this circle includes the secretaries of defense and state, the under secretaries and assistant secretaries of those two departments, the director of the Central Intelligence Agency, the chairman and members of the Joint Chiefs of Staff, the president's national security adviser, and key advisers of the president's choosing. Most of these officials are represented on the National Security Council (NSC), which was founded in 1947 by the same act that established an independent Air Force, the Defense Department, and the Central Intelligence Agency.

The rationale behind the establishement of the NSC was to centralize decision-making on national security issues, to ensure that the political and military strands of foreign policy issues would be more related to one another than formerly, and make certain that the major foreign policy advisers would be included in the decision-making process. Under Franklin D. Roosevelt, the decision on which high official or agency to include in a specific decision and which not to consult was entirely in the hands of the president. The NSC was supposed to be a check against such presidential discretion. Specifically, the members of the NSC are the president, the vice-president, the secretaries of defense and state, the directors of the CIA and the Office of Emergency Preparedness, the national security adviser, and the chairman of the Joint Chiefs of Staff. In 1976, Congress overrode a presidential veto and made the secretary of the treasury a member of the NSC in an explicit recognition of the extent to which foreign and domestic policy-making are becoming intertwined. Upon taking office, Jimmy Carter also added the chairman of the Council of Economic Advisers to the council.

Most recent presidents have circumvented the NSC as the formal or actual locus of foreign policy decision-making. Instead, they have formed their own informal circle of advisers whose membership may be somewhat broader than the statutory membership of the NSC. This is not to say that the *actors* who constitute the NSC are not in the president's own special circle; on the contrary, most of them usually are. Rather, we are arguing that: (1) Membership on the NSC does not guarantee an actor a place in the informal circle; and (2) actors not on the NSC but whom the president is close to may very well be included. The chief executive has a great deal of leeway in deciding whom to include. Kennedy included his brother, Attorney General Robert Kennedy, as well as staff aides Theo-

dore C. Sorenson and Arthur M. Schlesinger, Jr. Lyndon
Johnson relied upon such White House staff members as John
Roche and also consulted men of extensive backgrounds in
foreign relations who had no formal positions in the government. Perhaps the most prominent member of this group of
"wise men" was former Secretary of State Dean Acheson.
Nixon, on the other hand, has kept his inner circle more restricted. Dominating virtually all others has been Henry Kissinger, the national security adviser from 1969 to 1973 and
thereafter the secretary of state, although Attorney General
John Mitchell was reportedly consulted on occasions during
Nixon's first term. Gerald R. Ford relied almost exclusively on
Kissinger. His successor, Carter, however, had a larger inner
circle: Secretary of State Cyrus Vance, National Security adviser Zbigniew Brzezinski, United Nations ambassador Andrew Young, and CIA Director Stansfield Turner. Brzezinski,
like Kissinger and Roche, was recruited from the academic
community. He and Vance had served with Carter as members of the Trilateral Commission. Young, who first rose to
national attention as a civil rights activist and then became the
first black Representative from the South elected since Recon-
strution, was one of Carter's earliest supporters in his presiden-
tal campaign. Turner and Carter were classmates at the U.S.
Naval Academy.

Why have not most recent presidents made greater use of
the NSC? The answer is relatively simple. The act that created
the NSC attempted to *impose* an inner circle on the president
by granting various actors *ex officio* entry. Nevertheless, most
presidents simply did not accept the idea that they *had* to
consult certain actors and *only* those actors on foreign policy
questions. They wanted to include in the inner circle close
personal advisers and others whose opinions they respected.
Furthermore, no president has been equally close to all members of the NSC. Indeed, few have been close to their vice-
presidents at all. The vice-presidential candidate is usually
chosen more for his vote-getting ability than for his ability to
succeed the president. Vice-presidents have not played a major role in foreign policy. The inner circle thus provides the
president with a less formal means of accomplishing the same
basic goal as the NSC—formulation of major foreign policy

decisions. Thus high-level officials have not been systematically excluded from the decision-making process since the Roosevelt Administration.

The informal circle is especially prominent in crisis decision-making. This is where the alternatives are discussed and either accepted or rejected. The tendency of certain office-holders to remain in the inner circle from administration to administration (the secretaries of defense and state, the director of the CIA, the national security adviser, and the chairman of the Joint Chiefs of Staff) derives from their functions. They are the men charged with carrying out presidential decisions and thus can hardly be excluded from participating in the formulation of the decisions. However, being a member of this circle does not automatically imply that all advisers are equally influential. Truman and Eisenhower relied far more heavily on their secretaries of state—Acheson and John Foster Dulles, respectively—than on their secretaries of defense. Nixon and, to a lesser extent, Kennedy played down the role of the secretary of state. Nixon relied primarily on Kissinger, while Kennedy depended upon his secretary of defense. Indeed, Robert S. McNamara, who was secretary of defense under both Kennedy and Johnson, was among the closest and most persuasive advisers to each president until his opposition to the conduct of the Vietnam War alienated him from Johnson. Even then, Johnson did not stop listening to McNamara. Rather, the secretary was no longer "first among equals." The chairman of the Joint Chiefs of Staff, Earle G. Wheeler, found that his leverage with the president increased as McNamara's declined.

High-ranking officials in the inner circle often find themselves in dual roles when advising the president. On the one hand, they were selected by the president to advise him. On the other hand, as representatives of their agencies or departments they come into meetings of the inner circle with a point of view at least partially shaped by their daily experiences in more mundane situations. The secretary of state is faced with problems of diplomacy, while the secretary of defense is more concerned in his daily routine with questions of military strategy. Each may be faced with a dilemma of either expressing his own advice to the president or representing his department. Often there is no conflict between the two roles.[3] How-

ever, the institutional environments of the various agencies
can easily compel such a choice. Kennedy chose McNamara as
secretary of defense because of his success in applying modern
management techniques at the Ford Motor Company. He expected the secretary to apply the same techniques of measur-
ing cost-effectiveness to the Pentagon. The new secretary
immediately ran into problems with the heads of the various
services, who resented the attempt by a civilian—and an out-
sider to the Pentagon at that—to tell the military what its
organization and strategy should be. He battled with the services throughout his tenure as he took on more the role of
presidential adviser than representative of his agency. John
Foster Dulles, similarly, never bothered to penetrate into the
daily workings of the State Department, choosing instead to
represent his own views before Eisenhower. Acheson, in contrast, found little difficulty in adjusting to *both* roles in his
tenure under Truman as he tended to articulate to positions of
the State Department, which he had often helped to form.
Nixon, by contrast, viewed the position of secretary of defense
as less an advisory than a managerial post. In 1973, he selected
Elliot Richardson, secretary of health, education, and welfare,
to run the Pentagon. Richardson was soon shifted to the Justice
Department. He was, quite simply, a superb administrator
who could cut through organizational red tape and assert his
command position. When a department needed reorganizing,
he was Nixon's choice to head it. He later served as secretary
of commerce under Ford and accepted a diplomatic position
offered by Carter in early 1977.

Despite the fact the presidential styles are the basic determi-
nant of how the inner circle will be composed, some continui-
ties can be found throughout the post-World War II
presidencies. As we have noted, no president has relied heavily
on his vice-president. Each president will include in his innermost circle, although not in the NSC, several key members of
Congress, notably those on the Armed Services and Foreign
Relations Committees. Truman relied heavily upon Republican Senator ARthur Vandenberg (Mich.) for support for his
bipartisan foreign policy. Eisenhower, faced with a Democratic congressional majority during six of his eight years in
office and a hostile Republican majority during the other two,

paid great heed to the advice of Democratic floor leader Lyndon Johnson (Tex.). Kennedy was close to Fulbright, but had an unbreakable commitment to House Armed Services chairman Carl Vinson (D., Ga.). Vinson had almost forced himself into the president's innermost circle. A strong domestic conservative during his many years in Congress, he shifted ground under Kennedy and supported the president's domestic program in return for increased influence on military policy, particularly the defense budget. Johnson relied heavily upon the advice of two members of the Senate Armed Services Committee, with whom he had served while in that chamber: chairman Richard Russell (D., (Ga.) and the second-ranking Democrat, John Stennis (Miss.). Nixon, facing a Democratic Congress throughout his administration, relied upon Stennis (then chairman of the committee) and Senator Henry Jackson (D., Wash.). Indeed, Nixon had offered the position of secretary of defense to Jackson, but the Senator turned it down to pursue his own political career (including an abortive try for the Democratic nomination to run against Nixon in 1972).

Since Kennedy raided the Harvard faculty in 1961, there has also been a steady stream of academics into the president's inner circle. Some, like Kissinger under Eisenhower, Kennedy, Johnson, and Nixon, have been informal advisers and also held official governmental positions dealing with foreign policy. Others have occupied other executive positions, such as Schlesinger under Kennedy and Roche under Johnson, in which their functions were not limited to foreign policy. Despite Kennedy's widespread use of nationally recognized academics such as Schlesinger, McGeorge Bundy, John Kenneth Galbraith, and Roger Hilsman, and the continuation of this policy by Johnson, no academic appears to have made the mark upon policy formation and public opinion that Kissinger has under Nixon and Ford. The rationale for bringing academics into the policy-making process was highlighted in the Kennedy Administration: The academic community is a specialist in information and policy analysis, including drawing conclusions from the past, commodities that are essential for informed decision-making. Furthermore, academics are not tied to institutional loyalties in the same way that bureaucrats (including secretaries and department heads) are. They can therefore bring an independent perspective to the policy-making process.[4] While many academicians have filled positions in the bureaucracy or have been consulted by it, the tendency has been to appoint such men special advisers to the president.

When an administration changes, a change in the top-level foreign policy positions generally occurs. This does not mean, however, that the inner circle changes dramatically from one administration to another. Rather, members of the inner circle tend to be "in-and-outers," to hold one position in one administration and a different one in another.[5] Perhaps the best example is W. Averell Harriman, who served every Democratic president since Roosevelt. During the eight years of the Eisenhower Administration, he was not in the inner circle. The most common type of "in-and-outer" is the man who has served only when his party held the White House. When a change of party occurs, he will return to private life, most likely as either a businessman or an academic. Many academics do not go back to universities but take positions with "think tanks," such as the Brookings Institution, the Center for the Study of Democratic Institutions, the Rand Corporation, and the Hudson Institute. Indeed, Brookings is often considered a kind of "government in exile" for Democrats when their party is out of power.

The "in-and-outers" help bring continuity to foreign policy decision-making, so that the policy will not change radically from one administration to another. Johnson relied very heavily on a council of "wise men" with whom he regularly discussed major foreign policy questions. Included in this group were Acheson, Harriman, Cyrus Vance (formerly deputy secretary of defense), General Maxwell Taylor (chairman of the Joint Chiefs of Staff under Kennedy and ambassador to Vietnam for Johnson), and United Nations ambassador Arthur Goldberg. Not every "in-and-outer," however, has served only one party, several, including Kissinger, Henry Stimson, John McCloy, and Allen Dulles have served presidents of both parties. This is another factor in the continuity of foreign policy decisions from one administration to the next: the lack of partisanship on foreign policy.

Perhaps no president has relied as heavily on adivsers who served previous administrations as Carter. In 1976, he ran as a candidate opposed to the "Washington establishment"; in 1977, however, the new president appointed foreign policy advisers who were prominent members of that establishment! Vance and Brzezinski were the most prominent former members of the Kennedy and Johnson Administrations. Secretary of Defense Harold Brown, Treasury Secretary Michael Blumenthal, Charles Schultze of the Council of Economic Advisers, and arms control head Paul Warnke also had been part of what the press called the "junior varsity" of the earlier Democratic administrations. Schultze returned to the government from Brookings, as did many lesser officials. Harriman and Clark Clifford, who succeeded McNamara as secretary of defense under Johnson, served as presidential advisers. Carter also sought the counsel of men who had served Republican administrations, including Richardson and Ellsworth Bunker. The "new faces" promised by Carter during the 1976 presidential campaign were domestic policy advisers. In the "intermestic" area of energy policy, however, Carter's chief adviser was James Schlesinger, former defense secretary under Ford. Whatever changes in the decision-making process do occur with changes in administrations are due more to each president's style than to the changes he makes in personnel. Kennedy, for example, did not have a single inner circle for all issues. Rather, he selected different advisers for different problem areas. Nixon, on the other hand, has almost reduced the circle to himself and Kissinger. The mechanism of the NSC ensures that the circle will always be relatively permeable by at least those charged with the formal tasks of foreign policy formation. How successful each member is depends ultimately upon his relationship with his superior, the president.

THE SECOND CIRCLE: BUREAUCRATS AND ADVISERS

While the secretaries of state and defense—and often their under secretaries and assistant secretaries—and the director of the CIA are attending meetings of the president's inner circle, one may wonder, "Who's minding the store?" Each department has a set of lower-level leaders—deputy assistant secretaries and other officials. There are also the ambassadors under the wing of the State Department (including the ambassador to the United Nations) and the military and civilian officials in the Army, Navy, and Air Force in the Pentagon. There are also the agencies in limbo—independent of state, defense, or the CIA—but nowhere near matching the political clout of any of the three. These less powerful foreign policy bureaucracies include the Arms Control and Disarmament Agency (ACDA); the United States Information Agency (USIA); the Agency for International Development (AID); the military services; and the scientific and academic advisers to the president and the major foreign policy bureaucracies. Among these advisers, for example, are the Rand Corporation, a "think tank" for scientists in California; the Harvard Center for International Affairs; and similar academic centers at Princeton, MIT, the University of California at Berkeley, and other major universities. Another set of actors in this second circle are cabinet members who are only partially concerned with foreign policy issues. The department of commerce plays a major role in all aspects of international trade as well as in matters of immigration. The Department of the Treasury is a key actor in such decisions as the devaluation of the dollar in the international money market and, of course, has an abiding interest in the cost of U.S. foreign policy. The Agriculture Department is consulted on such issues as wheat sales to the Soviet Union and China and the use of surplus commodities in the foreign aid program.

Compared to the inner circle, there is greater continuity among the lower-level officials. A new administration does not mean massive changes in the executive departments. In particular, the military service personnel are quite durable. The country desks at State, the scientists at the Pentagon, the small staff at ACDA, and many career diplomats who have obtained their posts by rising through the Foreign Service remain in place as the men at the top change. The second circle thus provides a continuing organizational basis for foreign policy decision-making at lower levels. However, the bureaucrats at the various country desks (e.g., the African desk, the Western Europe desk, etc.) at State and in the three services at Defense also develop vested interests to protect. They served in their departments before their respective secretaries, under secretaries, and assistant secretaries were appointed and have established their own "standard operating procedures." A change in the men at the top may mean at least a minor shake-up of bureaucratic procedures. The lower-level officials may attempt to resist such changes, as the services did under McNamara. If a member of the inner circle also is occupied with settling problems and conflicts in his own department, he faces the problem of presenting a unified departmental position to the White House.

The function of the second circle is to provide ideas and information on policy alternatives and to make policy recommendations that the members of the inner circle can discuss among themselves. The second circle also carries out the day-to-day operations of the nation's foreign and military policies. It does not play a direct role in crisis decision-making or even in most foreign policy decisions, but it serves the members of the inner circle by providing background information and analyses to decision-makers. In 1962, during the debate on sending American troops into Laos, the State Department's Bureau of Intelligence and Research, the Policy Planning staff of the CIA, and logistics experts connected with Defense all prepared studies for their respective department heads.[6]

How well the members of this second circle perform their informational functions may affect how influential their spokesmen in the inner circle are. The president wants accurate information and sound analysis from his principal advisers —who in turn must rely upon their departments. The State Department has fared less well than Defense in the role of providing key information to its top-level bureaucrats. The large bureaucracy at State, with vested interests in the country desks, leads activist presidents to circumvent the department in making foreign policy innovations. Because the department is compartmentalized into sections dealing with specific geographical areas *and* functional areas, there is the virtually insurmountable problem of coming up with a unified position on foreign policy. As is the case with Congress—or with the Agriculture Department, which is segmented by crop—there are simply too many vested interests in the department to achieve a consensus on what ought to be done and to arrive at one set of recommendations on how to do it. The policy statements that the secretary of state receives from his subordinates therefore often take a long time in writing and tend to be ambiguous and lacking in references to short-run consequences. On the other hand, the policy recommendations of Defense tend to be produced relatively quickly and be quite specific, taking into account the short-run and long-range consequences of the alternatives.[7] The Pentagon is not without its own vested interests: There are strong inter-service rivalries and, indeed, even vigorous intra-service rivalries (such as that between the Strategic and Tactical Air Commands in the Air Force). But the Defense Department's policy recommendations to the president are more specific than those of State because much of the rivalry among the services is found on the more basic questions of which weapons to build rather than how to use the weapons at the nation's disposal if necessary. Because the study of which weapons system to deploy is a "harder" science than the study of the behavior of actors in the international system, defense can make more precise statements than state. For the same reason, the views espoused by the Defense Department are more likely to be seen by the president as reliable because they appear more "scientific." Furthermore, if one of the services sharply disagrees with the recommendations of the secretary of defense, its Chief of Staff can state his objections directly to the president, for the Joint Chiefs of Staff are almost always in the inner circle. In contrast, the secretary of state *may* be the only representative of that department in the inner circle. Even if the under secretary and assistant secretaries are on occasion in the inner circle, they do not ordinarily have the same influence as the Joint Chiefs.

The difficulties State has in developing clear-cut policy proposals further weaken the stature of the department in the inner circle by leading activist presidents to assume the political functions of the department. This "pre-emption" further lowers departmental morale. As Henry T. Nash has stated, "To the extent that crises in Asia and the Middle East have been 'managed' by the president's White House staff, the skills of state have eroded through disuse."[8] As Kissinger himself argued before taking on his duties with the Nixon Administration:

Because management of the bureaucracy takes so much energy and precisely because changing course is so difficult, many of the most important decisions are taken by extra-bureaucratic means. Some of the most important decisions are kept to a very small circle while the bureaucracy happily continues working away in ignorance of the fact that decisions are being made, or the fact that a decision is being made in a particular area. One reason for keeping the decisions to small groups is that when bureaucracies are so unwieldy and when their internal morale becomes a serious problem, an unpopular decision may be fought by brutal means, such as leaks to the press or to congressional committees.[9]

We thus have a kind of "vicious circle" in which the ambiguous policy recommendations of State are rejected and in which this rejection leads to a further weakening of the power of state in the inner circle. The public image of State is a function of the department's performance, of what people believe it stands for, and of how the department is viewed in comparison with Defense. The public sees State as representing foreign interests—through the country desks—and as bringing a troubled world to the door of Amercian citizens. The department is frequently called "Foggy Bottom." Originally this term referred to the haze surrounding the department's building in a valley in the District of Columbia; in recent years, the term has been used to characterize the type of thinking in the department. The public's view of State is not one of admiration. Frances E. Rourke has noted that

... the nonmilitary sector of the foreign affairs bureaucracy has been on the defensive before the bar of public opinion, confronted with a deficit of public support rather than the surplus which the military ordinarily enjoys. Over virtually the entire period of the cold war the State Department had been in a precarious position with respect to its public image.[10]

On the other hand, "the military role exerts a symbolic appeal that is as rare among bureaucratic organizations in the United States as it is in other societies. The identification of the military with national pride and achievement—in a word, with patriotism—is a quite extraordinary bureaucratic resource—

setting the Defense Department apart from all other executive agencies in the country."[11]

While State is less powerful in the inner circle because of its weakness when compared to Defense, there are even weaker agencies in the second circle. The functions of ACDA overlap with those of State, which is concerned with overall political position of the United States, and Defense, which is charged with devising military strategy and evaluating the level and kind of armaments needed to defend the country. Therefore, the ACDA, small by comparison with State and a midget compared to the giant-sized Defense Department, must walk a very thin line between these agencies and at the same time serve the president. ACDA is hardly without any power or influence: Gerard C. Smith, its head, was the chief American negotiator at the Strategic Arms Limitations Talks (SALT) between the United States and the Soviet Union. However, it is probably not unfair to say that the views at Defense, State, and particularly the White House, and from certain senators like Jackson who are very concerned with arms negotiations, played a more important role in setting the parameters for the SALT talks than did those within ACDA.* Indeed, the proposals Smith would discuss with the Soviets were determined by a Verification Panel in Washington. This panel included the president, Kissinger, the chairman of the Joint Chiefs of Staff, and representatives of State, Defense, and the CIA. Carter, who stressed his commitment to a limitation on nuclear arms, believed that ACDA would be strengthened if it were once more headed by the man who would be the chief SALT negotiator. His choice of Warnke for the two positions met with considerable criticism from members of Congress, the military, and others who believed that the United States no longer had an overall strategic superiority over the Soviet Union.

The second circle thus provides decision-makers with information on policy questions. It also runs the bureaucracies

*In 1973 the Nixon Administration, in a move to centralize more foreign policy decision-making in the White House, discharged or transferred every senior official in ACDA, ordered a one-third cut in the agency's budget, and took away the chairmanship of the strategic arms limitations talks (SALT) with the Soviet Union from ACDA. This process took place from January to July of that year and represented an administrative decision to restrict the influence of an agency not considered tough enough on arms limitations.

which—in turn—gather the information for the mid-level offi-cials. This circle has its own sphere of decision-making as well, but its decisions concern more routine types of foreign policy questions, which the president and his inner circle have nei-ther the time nor the inclination to answer. Will the adminis-tration agree to a particular request for foreign aid? Will it send a trade mission to a newly emerging country? These are the questions usually reserved for the bureaucracies.

The distinction between the actors in the first and second circles is not clear-cut over all decisions on foreign policy ques-tions. Because the lines between the inner and second circles are porous, a sudden crisis in a remote area in the world can elevate a bureaucrat to the periphery of the inner circle or even directly into it. Or, just as one president may pay more attention to the recommendations of his secretary of state and another to his secretary of defense, different policy areas may find the same actors in different circles. On foreign policy decisions affecting Africa, Kennedy was particularly close to Assistant Secretary of State for African Affairs G. Mennen Wil-liams. However, Williams was not consulted on most other foreign policy decisions. Depending upon how important a president thinks a particular problem area is—Kennedy was quite interested in American relations with Africa—and how close the president is to a given adviser, that actor may or may not be in the inner circle on any decision or series of decisions. Under secretaries and assistant secretaries may thus on occa-sion be members of the inner circle. A president such as Nixon, who has centralized the foreign policy decision-making pro-cess more than his predecessors, is less likely to consult them. In such a situation, these actors remain in the second circle.

THE THIRD CIRCLE:
CONGRESS, POLITICAL PARTIES, INTEREST GROUPS

The third circle, Congress, the political parties, and pressure groups, is somewhat farther removed from the policy-making process than the second. In crisis situations, the third circle plays a minor role at best in the policy-making process. Con-gress has been traditionally weak in the area of foreign policy, partisan cleavages are relatively rare, and interest groups simply have little at stake in most foreign policy decisions. Yet when certain foreign policy decisions have an impact upon domestic policies, the actors in this third circle play a more important role in the policy-making process. We shall examine each set of actors in turn.

Congress

The striking fact about Congress vis-à-vis the presidency in foreign policy is the gap between its formal powers and actual influence. Formally, both houses must pass any legislation connected with any foreign policy moves, must appropriate money when, as is so often the case, money is required, and can investigate any executive departments concerned with foreign policy formulation and implementation. Resolutions of either or both houses may support presidential policy, suggest new commitments, or attempt to restrain him. The Senate must approve of treaties by a two-thirds vote and must confirm cabinet and high diplomatic and military appointments. But whereas the president has far greater authority than one would judge from the powers allocated to him in the Constitution, Congress has far less influence than one might judge from its formal powers.

The old axiom "The president proposes, the Congress disposes" applies most strikingly in the area of foreign policy. On domestic policy, there are many cases in which legislation originates within the Congress. The role of Congress in foreign policy decision-making is essentially that of accepting, modifying, or rejecting executive policies. Rarely does Congress reject a policy, even in recent years when the House and Senate have made major efforts to become major actors in foreign policy decisions. Normally, the Congress legitimates executive policy in its original or some amended form and the *substance* of the policy is not altered much.[12] Since World War II, the record of executive dominance on foreign policy runs from the Truman Doctrine and the Marshall Plan, through Nixon's SALT I treaty (on ABMs) and his initiatives toward the Peoples' Republic of China and Ford's guarantee of 200 American civilian technicians to supervise the 1975 interim Sinai accord be-

TABLE 3-1. Congressional Involvement and Decision Characteristics*

	Congressional Involvement (High, Low, None)	Initiator (Congress or Executive)	Predominant Influence (Congress or Executive)	Legislation or Resolution (Yes or No)	Violence at Stake (Yes or No)	Decision Time (Long or Short)
1. Neutrality Legislation, the 1930s	High	Exec	Cong	Yes	No	Long
2. Lend-Lease, 1941	High	Exec	Exec	Yes	Yes	Long
3. Aid to Russia, 1941	Low	Exec	Exec	No	No	Long
4. Repeal of Chinese Exclusion, 1943	High	Cong	Cong	Yes	No	Long
5. Fulbright Resolution, 1943	High	Cong	Cong	Yes	No	Long
6. Building the Atomic Bomb, 1944	Low	Exec	Exec	Yes	Yes	Long
7. Foreign Service Act of 1946	High	Exec	Exec	Yes	No	Long
8. Truman Doctrine, 1947	High	Exec	Exec	Yes	No	Long
9. The Marshall Plan, 1947–48	High	Exec	Exec	Yes	No	Long
10. Berlin Airlift, 1948	None	Exec	Exec	No	Yes	Long
11. Vandenberg Resolution, 1948	High	Exec	Cong	Yes	No	Long
12. North Atlantic Treaty, 1948–49	High	Exec	Exec	Yes	No	Long
13. Korean Decision, 1950	None	Exec	Exec	No	Yes	Short
14. Japanese Peace Treaty, 1952	High	Exec	Exec	Yes	No	Long
15. Bohlen Nomination, 1953	High	Exec	Exec	Yes	No	Long
16. Indo-China, 1954	High	Exec	Cong	No	Yes	Short
17. Formosan Resolution, 1955	High	Exec	Exec	Yes	Yes	Long
18. International Finance Corporation, 1956	Low	Exec	Exec	Yes	No	Long
19. Foreign Aid, 1957	High	Exec	Exec	Yes	No	Long
20. Reciprocal Trade Agreements Act, 1958	High	Exec	Exec	Yes	No	Long
21. Monroney Resolution, 1958	High	Cong	Cong	Yes	No	Long
22. Cuban Decision, 1961	Low	Exec	Exec	No	Yes	Long

*The assignment of each case to different categories represents a "judgment" rather than a "calculation" on the part of the author. Admittedly the vignettes presented earlier in this chapter do not always reveal the bases or data for these classifications.

SOURCE: James A. Robinson, Congress and Foreign Policy-Making, rev. ed. (Homewood, Ill.: Dorsey, 1967), p. 65.

tween Israel and Egypt, to Carter's support for black majority rule in southern Africa. Congress has followed this executive leadership largely because it has agreed with the policies followed by the presidents. James A. Robinson has documented this presidential supremacy in a table through the early Kennedy—and "pre-Vietnam"—period (Table. 3.–1). Not until recent years has this pattern changed at all. What is especially significant was the almost complete absence, until the 1970s, of congressional initiative in the key area of the possible or actual use of force.

The major exception in the post-World War II period was the Indochina crisis of 1954. This was due to President Eisenhower's indecisiveness—or unwillingness—about whether or not to intervene after the battle of Dien Bien Phu had turned against the French. Eisenhower had been elected to get the country out of Korea, and he was thus politically in a poor position to involve the country in another land war in Asia despite his own perception of high American stakes in Vietnam. He also questioned whether the United States could avoid identification with French colonialism. His secretary of state and chairman of the Joint Chiefs of Staff were, however, strongly inclined to intervene with air strikes. Eisenhower sent them to the "Hill" where, upon questioning, it became clear that our European allies had not been consulted (the administration knew the British were opposed) and that the army was vigorously opposed. In these circumstances, congressional leaders expressed their reluctance about unilateral American intervention. Eisenhower therefore decided against intervention (or else was against the intervention to start with and used the Congress to cool off his advisers).[13] But this does not mean that Eisenhower paid greater respect to the constitutional requirements; rather, his obeisance to Congress legitimated his decision not to act, whether originally he was for or against the intervention.

Let us suppose that Eisenhower had been determined to intervene. He then presumably would have done what he did in 1955, when he decided to defend Quemoy and Matsu in the Straits of Formosa—ask Congress for a resolution of approval *after* he had told congressional leaders that in his judgment intervention was necessary. There is no reason to doubt that

Congress would have gone along. President Nixon, another Republican and Eisenhower's vice-president, has reverted to the Truman tradition, and then some; he, like Truman in Korea, felt that he had all the necessary authority to conduct the war in Vietnam as he saw fit but, while Truman at least listened to congressional opinions even if he did not always act upon them, Nixon rarely consulted congressional leaders or listened to their advice.

It was Johnson's Under Secretary of State, Nicholas Katzenbach, who argued that the congressional power to declare war had been outmoded by the nuclear age when the only wars "safe" to fight were limited wars. In responding to senatorial complaints that the Gulf of Tonkin resolution had not given the president the right to send American divisions to South Vietnam and American planes winging north to drop their bombs, Katzenbach asserted that the Tonkin resolution "fully fulfills the obligation of the executive in a situation of this kind to participate with the Congress, to give the Congress full and effective voice, the functional equivalent of the Constitutional obligation expressed in the provision of the Constitution with respect to declaring war."*

While institutionally the Congress has the authority to declare war and raise and maintain the armed forces, practically all the decisions to use or not use military force are made by the president. The issue of congressional versus executive control over foreign and military policies has existed since the administration of George Washington, because the lines of demarcation between executive and legislative powers are unclear and, in fact, as has been noted frequently, invite a struggle for the control of American foreign policy. The outcome of

*For the pros and cons of this issue, as well as Katzenbach's testimony, see "The Legislative-Executive Foreign Policy Relationship in the 90th Congress," *Congressional Digest* (October, 1968). If an atmosphere of suspicion had not hung over the Tonkin resolution, a belief that the administration had hurried the Congress and not told the full story—that the first attack by North Vietnamese torpedo boats on the American destroyer might have occurred because Hanoi perhaps surmised a relationship between these operations and the nearby operations of South Vietnamese patrol boats, and that it remained questionable whether a second attack on two American destroyers two days later had in fact occurred—the Katzenbach argument would have had more force to it, because Congress could not then claim that it was innocent of what was going on in Vietnam as it pretended later when it sought to get off the presidential bandwagon after the war had turned sour.

this struggle and Congress's recognition of its institutional impotency on the issue of war and peace in a century in which the United States has increasingly been drawn into preserving the balance of power in Europe, twice against Germany and once against Soviet Russia, is evident in the repeated but vain attempts to restrain the president: in the 1930s, the neutrality legislation; in the 1950s the Bricker amendment (never passed); and, since Vietnam, efforts ranging from the National Commitments Resolution, stating that American commitments need executive *and* legislative approval, to the War Powers Act making it mandatory for the president to seek congressional approval for the use of force after sixty days.

During the Vietnam War, there were a series of attempts to cut off funds for the use of American troops in neighboring nations and to require troops in Vietnam to return home. Several passed the Senate, but were rejected by the House of Representatives. An amendment to forbid funding for military operations in Cambodia did pass both houses, but by that time the troops were already out. The only real success of a congressional amendment to terminate the American involvement in Vietnam occurred *after* the Paris peace agreement, when all U.S. forces had been withdrawn from Vietnam and all prisoners returned to America. Only then did the Congress cut off funds for the administration's continued bombing in Cambodia, where no cease-fire had yet occurred. Yet, the legislative success was qualified, because Nixon vetoed the appropriations bill to which the cut-off on funds had been attached. The president's need for funds for several executive agencies led to a compromise delaying the end of bombing for several weeks. This gave Washington and Hanoi another chance to negotiate a Cambodian cease-fire and await the onset of the monsoon season, which would make further fighting very difficult.

In the wake of Vietnam and Watergate, when presidential power had come under sharp attack, congressional concern over its role in the shaping of foreign policy reached new heights. In April and May, 1975, the House rejected administration attempts to save the tottering regime in South Vietnam. Ford received another setback when Congress voted to bar military aid to Turkey in the aftermath of the invasion of

Cyprus by the Turks and still another in January, 1976, when the House concurred in a Senate decision to prohibit military aid to the pro-Western factions in the Angolan civil war. This heightened concern for foreign policy in the Congress is also reflected in the intensive questioning the Senate Foreign Relations committee gave Kissinger before approving the interm Sinai accord, the establishment of temporary committees to investigate the CIA in 1976 and making the committees permanent for the 95th Congress (1977–78), and the withdrawal of Sorenson as the nominee for CIA director by Carter in January, 1977, when it became obvious that a majority of the members of both parties on the Senate Intelligence Committee opposed him.

The extent of this newfound congressional "power" should not, however, be overestimated. In the cases of the Vietnam and Angola military assistance, Ford had little support among the mass public and the Congress was reflecting a more fundamental disagreement with the president. Support for Angolan military aid could not be obtained among any major group (Northern Democrats, Southern Democrats, or Republicans) in either the House or the Senate. The Turkish situation was somewhat more complicated. On the one hand, the arms involved would possibly be used against another NATO ally, Greece, and there is a much larger Greek-American population (which generally votes Democratic, the party in control of Congress) than a Turkish-American group. On the other hand, Turkey had not been cooperative with the United States on restricting the growth of poppy seeds, the source of heroin. On issues where public support for the president was greater, Congress was more cooperative. After grilling Kissinger on the details of the Sinai accord, the Senate Foreign Relations committee sent the agreement to the full chamber, where it was overwhelmingly approved. Few observers believed that either intelligence committee would have lasting impact on the conduct of foreign policy. What changes in intelligence operations might occur were attributed to the revelations of the press rather than the operations of either committee. There was little cooperation between the House and the Senate committees. Indeed, many observers felt that the major concern of each committee chairman was the seeking of higher office:

Sen. Frank Church (D., Idaho) made an unsuccessful attempt to obtain his party's presidential nomination, but Rep. Otis Pike (D., N.Y.) resisted the temptation to give up his safe House seat in order to enter the crowded Senate primary in his home state.

Congress, then, has indeed become more assertive in the area of foreign policy, but it is still far weaker than the executive. This is particularly the case with respect to proposing alternative policies. Why is this so?

First, there is the stark contrast in capabilities between the nation's chief diplomat and commander-in-chief and the legislative branch. The president, nationally elected, is the national spokesman; Congress represents local interests and, because the congressman may wish to be re-elected, these interests tend to take priority over national considerations. The president can act quickly; Congress, as a deliberative body, is supposed to take its time and usually is only able to act slowly. The president has vast amounts of information; Congress is usually dependent for its information upon the executive. But even when Congress obtains what it needs through administration witnesses, staff investigation, and so forth, the rapidity of events often means that by the time it collects the necessary information, the president has already acted. A Republican spokesman remarked in the heyday of bipartisan cooperation after World War II that

> . . . the trouble is that these "crises" never reach Congress until they have developed to a point where congressional discretion is pathetically restricted. When things finally reach the point where a president asks us to "declare war" there usually is nothing left except to "declare war."[14]

The president may also often need to act secretly, as during World War II, so that the enemy does not obtain useful information, or since then during cease-fire negotiations with a limited war adversary, which cannot be conducted in full public view, or contacts with his Russian opposite numbers during crises or at times of impasse in negotiations, or to explore the establishing of more normal relations with countries e.g., with China in 1970–71 or Cuba in 1974–75. Congress is more like a sieve with frequent leaks of information (not that executive departments do not leak, but knowledge of secret negotiations can be limited to a very few participants).

In addition, Congress does its work in committees. A problem arises from the multiplicity of committees involved in some aspect of foreign affairs. Besides the broad area of foreign relations, committees concern themselves with such other areas as armed services, appropriations, commerce, government operations, banking, agriculture, immigration, and space and science. Moreover, these committees exist in both houses. (See Table 3-2.) Thus there is no single place within Congress, or, for that matter, in either house, to pull all the pieces together. Each committee has only a partial view of the broader foreign policy picture. There is no point at which the divergent perspectives and interests of, for example, the military and nonmilitary programs can be balanced against one another, or, even more important, domestic claims can be compared to foreign policy requirements. There is only one such point in the government at present: the presidency.[15]

The disorganization of Congress is highlighted by a critical overlapping of functions in the most fundamental power of the legislative body: the power of the purse. Substantive committees—such as Foreign Relations in the Senate and Foreign Affairs in the House for foreign aid and Armed Services in both houses on the defense budget—set upper limits on the amount of money that can be spent on these programs, which fall within their jurisdictions. These limits are called *authorizations.* The authorizations are then sent to the House and Senate Appropriations committees to determine the actual amount of money a program will receive. Until recently, Congress has played a docile role on the defense budget. If it took any action at all, it was to restore administration cuts in the allocations requested by the various services. In fiscal year 1961, the Congress actually increased the president's budget request for military spending by almost 2 percent. The executive advantage in the budgeting process is due to two factors: (1) the greater manpower (and thus information) that the executive has for determining the defense budget, including the staffs of the Pentagon and the Office of Management and Budget, compared to the combined total of sixty members of the

TABLE 3-2. Committees Of Congress Dealing With Foreign Policy Issues

Committee	Subjects
Foreign Relations (Senate)	General conduct of foreign policy; declarations of war; treaties
International Relations (House)	Same as Senate Foreign Relations, except treaties
Armed Services (Senate and House)	Military affairs; defense budget
Interstate and Foreign Commerce (House)	Transportation, shipping, telecommunications
Commerce, Science, and Transportation (Senate)	Telecommunications, space program, tourism
Appropriations (Senate and House)	All programs requiring funding; defense budget; budget for running bureaucracies
Budget (Senate and House)	Determines overall spending levels by the Congress
Banking, Housing, and Urban Affairs (Senate)	International monetary policy; international commerce; authorizations for Export-Import bank
Banking and Currency (House)	International monetary policy; authorizations for Export-Import bank
Intelligence (Senate and House)	Oversight of intelligence agencies
Science and Technology (House)	Space program
Ways and Means (House)	
Finance (Senate)	Reciprocal trade agreements; tariffs
Public Works (House)	
Environment and Public Works (Senate)	Environment; atomic energy
Interior and Insular Affairs (House)	
Energy and National Resources (Senate)	Energy legislation; environment
Agriculture (Senate and House)	Price supports; international food policy
Rules (House)	Setting of legislative agenda for House bills
Governmental Affairs (Senate)	General oversight; nuclear export policy
Government Operations (House)	General oversight; oversight on trade relations (including Arab embargo of Israel)

two authorizing committees (forty-five Armed Services members in the House, only fifteen in the Senate) and eighty-one members of the two appropriating committees (fifty-five and twenty-six members, respectively); and (2) the lack of coordination in the processes of authorization and appropriations. There is little overlapping membership on authorizing and appropriating committees in the Senate, while none is allowed in the House.

The "reform" establishing a congressional budgetary process does add some degree of order to the chaos, but it also creates yet a third committee in each chamber which considers funds for any foreign policy legislation.[16] In 1974 the House attempted a major committee reorganization. Too many "interests" were affected, however, and the plan failed.[17] A similar plan was proposed in the Senate in 1977 and it fell prey to the same objections raised in the House. Some reorganization was accomplished, the most notable aspect being the creation of a comprehensive energy committee (while Carter was proposing an Energy Department).

This decentralization of power in the budgetary process permits the military services to appeal to the budget, authorizing, and appropriations committees independently to argue against cuts made either by the White House or by another committee. As criticism of the war increased, however, so did congressional concern with the defense budget. Formerly a court of last resort for the aggrieved services, the legislative branch in 1968 suddenly reversed itself and became the great budget-cutter on funds for procurement of weapons. From 1959 to 1967, Congress had never cut the president's procurement requests by more than 4 percent. In 1968 and 1969, the congressional reductions approached 15 percent![18] This pattern continued until 1976, when charges that the Soviet Union might be gaining strategic superiority over the United States led to an increase by Congress in military spending for arms procurement. Nevertheless, the Congress continued to maintain some degree of independence by opposing *specific* projects favored by the administration, such as the B-1 bomber. Even on the B-1 bomber, the legislative branch did not cut off all funding. The renewed congressional interest in foreign policy decision-making, while continuing to let the executive make the "critical" decisions, is typified by a recent law requiring legislative approval of foreign arms sales over $5000: Nothing was done to prevent companies from taking advantage of the "loophole" allowing larger purchases to be billed in multiple quantities of $4999.99!

Political Parties

In contrast to many parliamentary systems, the political party system in the United States has not been marked by either ideologically distinct or internally cohesive legislative parties. Most roll call votes in the House of Commons in Great Britain are along strictly party lines. Indeed, a member who deviates from the party position can be thrown out of the party, although this rarely happens in practice. In the United States, however, the only votes that can be safely predicted to come out along strictly partisan lines are those that choose the leaders of each house of Congress.

Nevertheless, on domestic policies that are primarily distributive—general appropriations measures, agriculture price supports, public works bills, legislation relating to the size of the bureaucracy and the overall level of government spending, and (until recently) military appropriations measures— party unity has been relatively strong. these issue areas involve the spending of money by the government and find the Democrats as the "big spenders" and the Republicans as the "guardians of the nation's purse." The differences between the parties on distributive issues are quite real: In five of the 12 Congresses from 1947 to 1970, a majority of House Democrats found themselves voting contrary to a majority of House Republicans on *every* distributive roll call that generated any controversy at all![19] As occurred during Korea, the extent of partisan voting declined sharply during the period of American involvement in Vietnam. A sharp increase, returning to pre-Vietnam levels, occurred after the withdrawal of American troops from Southeast Asia and continues to mark domestic policy-making in the Congress.[20]

In contrast, those votes that involve "winners" and "losers" —either domestically or in terms of foreign policy—have tended to produce legislative coalitions that cut across party lines. Such redistributive measures as civil rights legislation, antipoverty measures, proposals to increase the minimum wage, and the like have produced only *one* roll call from 1947 to 1970, on which 90 percent of the Democrats opposed 90 percent of the Republican members of the House.[21] Redistributive policies are matters of broad ideological concern that follow regional more closely than partisan lines. On such policies, a "conservative coalition" of Southern Democrats and Republicans opposes a more liberal group of Northern Democrats and a few Northeastern Republicans. On foreign policy questions, there is a rather different pattern of cleavage from that on either distributive or redistributive domestic policies. Foreign policy votes rarely produce strong partisan cleavages. Rather, such roll calls have been bipartisan. Not a single roll call on a straightforward foreign policy vote during the twenty-four years from 1947 to 1970 found 80 percent of House Democrats opposing 80 percent of House Republicans.[22] Simple party majorities have been opposed to one another on foreign policy measures in many Congresses, but there appears to be no clear-cut pattern of consistency in partisan voting on foreign policy votes in Congress. As the overall level of party voting has increased since Vietnam, so has the extent of party conflict on foreign policy. It appears, however, that such voting patterns reflect a conflict between the president and Congress (particularly the congressional opposition party, which controlled a majority in each house) rather than a fundamental partisan division on the substance of foreign policy.

The aim of a bipartisan foreign policy, as previously discussed, was, in the words of Assistant Secretary of State for Congressional Relations Ernest A. Gross in 1949, "to make it virtually impossible for 'momentous divisions' to occur in our foreign affairs" and to provide a "continuity and consistency"[23] in decision-making from one administration to another. Franklin D. Roosevelt had moved toward a bipartisan foreign policy as early as 1940 by naming Republicans Henry Stimson and Frank Knox as secretaries of war and the navy, respectively. By appointing members of the opposition party to high-level government positions, Roosevelt sought to dramatize the idea that the stakes in foreign policy decision-making involved the welfare of the entire nation and transcended any partisan lines. Truman continued the bipartisan foreign policy after World War II. James Forrestal and Robert A. Lovett, both Republicans, served as secretary of defense under Truman, and Lovett also served as under secretary of state. Kennedy appointed McNamara as secretary of defense, William C. Foster as head of ACDA, John A. McCone as head of the CIA, and Henry Cabot Lodge as ambassador to Saigon—among others. Democrats have followed this pattern of bipartisanship more than the Republicans have, probably because Democratic presidents have been more concerned with warding off charges of being too "soft" toward Communist regimes than have Republicans (the charges, after all, have come mainly from Republicans). A Democratic administration with Republicans playing a major role in the formation of foreign policy, Democrats believed, would be less susceptible to such attacks. Indeed, John Foster Dulles negotiated the World War II peace treaty with Japan, while Senator Arthur Vandenberg (R., Mich.), chairman of the Senate Foreign Relations Committee, participated in American delegations to the United Nations, negotiating teams for the peace treaties with the Eastern European countries after World War II, and the establishment of the North Atlantic treaty Organization.

The appointment of opposition party members was just one way that presidents sought to gain bipartisan support for their foreign policy. Truman worked rather closely with Vandenberg, particularly during 1947–48, when the Republicans controlled Congress. The White House openly brought Congress into the decision-making process on foreign policy. The Marshall Plan and the establishment of NATO probably marked the high points of congressional involvement in foreign policy-making. Truman pursued a bipartisan foreign policy not only because he believed that the international stakes were extremely high and that they transcended partisan grounds, but also because his party simply did not have the strength in Congress to adopt his proposals. In 1947–48 particularly, cooperation with the Republicans was a necessity.

In this respect, Republican chief executives did resemble their Democratic counterparts. Eisenhower had to deal with a Democratic Congress during six of his eight years in the White House, and he found Senate Majority Leader Lyndon B.

Johnson's support of his foreign policy more dependable than that of his own party leaders. Democrats have generally been more cohesive on foreign policy votes in Congress than have Republicans. Furthermore, Eisenhower's dealings with his own party majority in 1953–54 were rather strained. Senator Robert Taft (R., Ohio) was Eisenhower's first majority leader; Taft had been Eisenhower's main competitor for the 1952 Republican nomination, and the two men sharply disagreed on foreign policy questions. Following Taft's death, the president received only slightly more support from Majority Leader William Knowland (R., Calif.), who had presidential ambitions of his own. In 1953, the bipartisan foreign policy of more than a decade was almost upset by the efforts of Republican Senator John W. Bricker (Ohio) to limit severely the president's authority to conduct foreign policy by amending the Constitution to prohibit the executive from entering into any agreement that committed American troops to any foreign conflict without express congressional approval. Knowland, in a rare spirit of cooperation with Eisenhower, agreed to be the floor leader for an administration-sponsored substitute to the Bricker amendment. Until recent years, bipartisan foreign policy was accentuated when control of the White House and Congress was split between the two parties. Indeed, it appeared that there would have to be a bipartisan foreign policy if the nation were to have any type of coherent foreign policy in a situation of divided control. When one party controls both the executive and legislative branches, as occurred from 1949 to 1955 and from 1961 to 1969, criticism of foreign policy may increase because bipartisan support is no longer strictly necessary; conversely, when the opposition controls Congress, it may well be reluctant to oppose the president outright, for he can then accuse it of subordinating the nation's interests to partisan politics and advantage. Yet a president cannot be sure in advance from which direction criticism will come. Eisenhower received the bulk of his criticism from fellow Republicans, Johnson from other Democrats. Kennedy and Truman, on the other hand, found their own parties more united in their support and the opposition split.

Partisanship, of course, has not been totally absent from foreign policy decision-making. The parties have traditionally divided over the size of the defense budget, with the Democrats supporting increases in military spending and the Republicans calling for cutbacks. This is not to suggest that the Democrats have been traditionally more "hawkish" than the Republicans. Rather, the Democrats have generally been more willing to support higher levels of expenditures *across the board* than have Republicans. Recent years have witnessed a strong reversal of this pattern of behavior. The defense budget is no longer viewed as just another part of the budget, but rather as a major element of the nation's foreign policy, as well as a key issue of foreign/domestic priorities. Another area of foreign policy that has often (though not always) divided the congressional parties is reciprocal trade legislation.[24] The Democrats have generally supported lower tariff barriers, with the Republicans taking the opposite position. However, recent years again indicate somewhat of a shift in this polarization. American companies have been hurt by many imported goods that are sold at prices below their own. Strong pressure from both labor and management has created a great deal of bipartisan support for more restrictive tariffs on many items. This support is not yet a protectionist coalition, but it does indicate that the old partisan coalitions are breaking down. By contrast, however, to the extreme degree of partisanship on Far Eastern policy after the fall of Nationalist China and the Korean War—with its accusations of the Democrats as not only stupid but treasonous—American foreign policy in Southeast Asia has drawn a rather different response. For the war in Vietnam aroused an opposition that crossed party lines, just as support for it did. Neither Johnson nor Nixon could count on the support of the Senate Democratic Majority Leader Mansfield as previous presidents could count on majority leaders in direct confrontations with Congress. Mansfield did not take a leadership role in the antiwar movement in the Senate, but he did openly criticize the Vietnam policies of both presidents.

When Nixon entered the White House in 1969, Democratic cohesion on the war issue was considerably strengthened. Many Democratic members of the House and the Senate who had felt constrained in criticizing the foreign policies of a president of their own party became fiercely partisan when the war effort could be blamed upon a Republican president. This increase in Democratic partisanship permitted a bipartisan coalition *opposing the president* to prevail on several antiwar measures. On the other hand, when a major foreign policy measure passed the House in the summer of 1973, the pattern of support for the measure found Democrats opposing the president's Cambodia policy and the Republicans supporting it. Two very different types of anti-presidential coalitions have formed: a partisan one in the House and a bipartisan one in the Senate. Opposition to the war in Indochina was found in *both* political parties in the Senate prior to 1969. Democratic members of the House, who are generally less assertive on foreign policy questions than their colleagues in the Senate, generally supported Johnson's policies in Indochina. When Nixon took office, Democrats in both houses became much more critical of the war. In the Senate, the addition of many new Democratic critics made the pre-1969 bipartisan coalition a major force. By 1973 the Senate produced large majorities in favor of restricting presidential dominance of foreign policy. The opposition that had developed in the House during this period was composed basically of Democrats. Since there was not a large antiwar group among Republican representatives before 1969, the antiwar coalition in the House was primarily partisan. With the president as chief foreign policymaker, however, either the bipartisan coalition in the Senate or the partisan one in the House has the potential to isolate itself still further from a policy-making role on foreign offices if it cannot find the means to assert some congressional influence on the decision process.

The critical question which now arises is: Can a Congress, overwhelmingly Democratic, of whom less than half have ever served under a chief executive of the same party, work with Carter on questions of foreign policy? And, conversely, we might ask: Can a president with no previous Washington experience and with a history of fighting with the legislative branch (during his term as governor of Georgia, 1971–1975) effectively work with an increasingly policy-oriented Democratic Congress? Behind both of these queries is the subtle reminder that in national elections, the Republicans do not win; the Democrats lose. The majority party has a registration and identification ratio of more than 2–1 over the GOP. And, since

World War II, the Democrats have lost the White House precisely when they divided over foreign policy. Will the electoral incentives be sufficient to create more cooperation between the Congress and the White House on foreign policy?

Interest Groups

In domestic politics in general and distributive politics in particular, the role of interest groups is quite strong. Farmers' lobbies have an important say on agriculture bills; veterans' organizations are forceful proponents of their demands for more government services; and business lobbies are rather successful in maintaining tax loopholes in the Internal Revenue Service code. In foreign policy, however, interest groups are less numerous and less powerful.

One critical reason why interest groups are weaker on foreign policy questions than on domestic policy is that lobbyists specialize in the provision of information to members of Congress and the bureaucracy. Spokesman for organized interests, Lester W. Milbrath has noted, "communicate to government what is happening or what is likely to happen to their clients. They advocate policies and points of view before both Congress and the executive agencies. They stimulate others to communicate with government."[15] If information is the lobbyist's basic resource, it is not difficult to see why interest groups are relatively powerless in foreign policy. As Milbrath states:

> Domestic policies often have direct economic consequences for citizens; these consequences are fairly easily demonstrable in a message. Foreign issues, on the other hand, usually have more indirect consequences . . . and it is difficult to demonstrate in a message how a group might be hurt.[26]

Indeed, the stakes in foreign policy appear once again to be quite different from those in domestic policy. But so is the problem of the interest group. On matters of domestic policy, the lobbyist may well have information that the bureaucrat or member of Congress does not have. The interest groups can generate their own sources of information on questions such as the effect of an increased minimum wage or of a restriction of agriculture price supports to $20,000 per farmer. On foreign policy questions, interest groups seem no better off than Congress in terms of the amount of information each has and in a considerably weaker position than either the State or the Defense Department.

The weakness of most pressure groups in foreign policy questions can be demonstrated by the example of reciprocal trade legislation—a foreign policy issue with strong domestic policy implications. Since a less restrictive tariff will lower the prices of many American products, and also because tariff legislation is one area of foreign policy decision-making in which affected groups might be expected to have a great deal of information to peddle to members of Congress and the executive branch, it might also be thought that interest group activity would be very strong on this type of legislation. Indeed, the larger corporations do make attempts to contact members of Congress on trade legislation; and the larger the business, the more likely it is that the company will have made some contact on Capitol Hill.[27]

However, they have tended to concentrate their efforts on members of Congress who agreed with their own stands. Free-trade supporters made contact with members of Congress with similar views; protectionist corporations spoke to protectionist members. Furthermore, the many corporations were just as likely to be opposed to one another as to present a unified front. Lower import duties on crude oil might have the support of the major oil firms but would be opposed by producers of alternative sources of energy, such as natural gas. On trade legislation, Raymond Bauer et al. have commented:

> The stereotype notion of omnipotent pressure groups becomes completely untenable once there are groups aligned on both sides. The result of opposing omnipotent forces is stalemate. But, even taken by themselves, the groups did not appear to have the raw material of great power. We noted shortages of money, men, information, and time.[28]

Indeed, many large companies acknowledged that a liberalized trade bill would help part of their business and harm part of it.

Another areas of foreign policy decision-making in which the role of interest groups might be presumed to be relatively strong is the defense budget. With an annual defense budge of over $70 billion, it is not unreasonable to assume that military contractors would attempt to play a major role in the defense budgetary process. And it is indeed the case that military contractors have supported specific services in their competition for funds and weapons. However, the alignment of specific contractors with specific services has intensified the interservice rivalry over the defense budget and allowed the president and the secretary of defense to exploit these divisions and gain a free hand in determining the broader questions of strategy —the levels of forces, the kinds of weapons, and how these weapons are to be used—on the basis of their perceptions of external threats and the level of technology rather than simply on the basis of military requests. Aaron Wildavsky has stated, "The outstanding feature of the military's participation in making defense policy is their amazing weakness. Whether policy decisions involve the size of the armed forces, the choice of weapons systems, the total defense budget, or its division into components, the military have not prevailed."[29] In 1961, Samuel Huntington noted that in the sharp competition among the services and the interest groups supporting them, the Department of Defense had 40,000 prime contractors.[30] If every one of them attempted to influence the defense budget—either through the services or directly—the result would probably have been a stalemate. The contractors not only seem to have little influence on the magnitude of the defense budget, but there is also little evidence to indicate that they carry great weight in the actual distribution of the shares. Even in the House Armed Services Committee, members have *not* received disproportionate shares in the awarding of prime military contracts.[31] Nor, despite a widespread myth to the contrary, has any systematic relationship been found between voting behavior of members of Congress on defense spending and either the level of military spending in a district or a state or the number of defense-related jobs in a district.[32] In part, these results may be a further indication of the relative weakness of Congress—at least until quite recently—in defense budgeting.

The "intermestic" policies of food and energy also involve group conflict, just as trade and the defense budget do. However, the policy-making process on these issues is considerably more complex. In addition to the range of domestic interest groups involved, there are also foreign actors who can restrict the range of alternative policies from which a decision can be made. There are also multinational corporations, such as the oil companies or telecommunications giants such as A.T.&T., I.T.T., or IBM, which operate both in the consuming nations (particularly the United States) and the producing nations (such as the OPEC countries). These corporations are, of course, among the domestic interests involved in the policy-making process—thus having a greater impact than might occur on most domestic policies. But multinational corporations are not easily controlled by the American government. They can act in concert with the producing nations (as the oil companies cooperate with the OPEC nations) and are not subject to United States regulations outside the American borders. Pharmaceutical firms can market products abroad which have not been approved by American authorities. The leverage that the United States has over such companies is limited, since the multinationals can threaten to move their bases of operation abroad. The policy-making process on these issues becomes much more complex—and, often the result is no coordinated policy at all.

On the broad ideological questions of foreign policy, there is evidence of interest group activity. Among the more notable groups are those with a distinct ideological orientation. On the left, there are the Committee for a Sane Nuclear Policy (SANE) and the Women's Strike for Peace, among others. On the right, the most famous group is the Committee of One Million, which for two decades fought American recognition of the Communist government in China. The committee had obtained considerable support in Congress after the Communist victory in China in 1949 and was viewed by State Department officials as highly influential in the 1950s and the early 1960s.[33] On the other hand, the influence of SANE has been virtually nil on policy formation. Yet the perceived influence of each group is hardly a function of the tactics normally associated with domestic interest groups: providing information, working in campaigns, and the like. Rather, the Committee of One Million was seen as effective because its position and the official position of the government were the same. When the government's position on China became somewhat more ambiguous during the mid-1960s, the committee virtually vanished overnight. SANE, on the other hand, had developed a long-standing reputation of opposing the foreign policies of the Eisenhower, Kennedy, Johnson, and Nixon Administrations. Its major emphasis during the 1950s and early 1960s was on multilateral, inspected disarmament; in the mid-1960s and the 1970s, the group became a leading opponent of the war in Vietnam. The proposal for unilateral initiatives on disarmament had created the impression that SANE was largely a fringe group, and, as opposition to the war in Vietnam increased, public officials who disagreed with administration policies sought to publicize their views through ad hoc organizations considered more legitimate than SANE. In 1966 Members of Congress for Peace Through Law, an informal organization, was established as a congressional vehicle to oppose the war in Indochina.

Perhaps the most influential type of interest group on foreign policy questions is the ethnic lobby. Some ethnic lobbies want very little from the actors in the decision-making arenas. An example is the typical Eastern European group (the Ukranians, Latvians, Lithuanians, and Estonians) who seek demonstrations of congressional support for freedom for their fellow countrymen who reside in formerly independent states that are now part of the Soviet Union. Such lobbyists may ask for little more than insertions into the *Congressional Record* of prepared speeches supporting their cause by members of the House and the Senate. These groups also are noticeable around the State Department, but they realize that they have no real chance to change American foreign policy toward the Soviet Union.

Other ethnic groups with somewhat more political clout are Jewish agencies lobbying for support for Israel and black groups urging support for African nations. Bernard C. Cohen has found that Jewish groups are the most active in the State Department.[34] Unlike the East European groups, the Jewish groups press for more than simple policy statements: They also lobby for weapons for Israel. And they are more successful than many other ethnic groups because politicians in areas in which the Jewish vote is large recognize that they might be in electoral trouble if they cannot produce concrete results regarding American policy toward Israel. More than one politician has been defeated in urban areas because he was accused of not being pro-Israeli. Indeed, William Haddad, a candidate in a Democratic primary for Congress in New York several years ago, was defeated when his opponent, incumbent Leonard Farbstein, stressed the fact that he had an Arab name— even though both candidates actually were Jewish! The Jewish vote is more of a bloc vote than the East European vote.

The strength of Jewish groups is not a new phenomenon in American politics. Ethnic groups have played a major role in foreign policy debates throughout the twentieth century. Irish groups, which disliked Britain intensely, argued against American participation in World War I and later opposed U.S. entry into the League of Nations. Italian and German groups were active opponents of American entry into both world wars. Indeed, Germanic groups were extremely powerful in the Midwest throughout the century, electing several senators and members of the House. While often quite liberal on domestic policies, the Midwestern members of Congress elected from districts with heavy concentrations of Germans were decidedly isolationist in their foreign policy. Their rationale for not fighting a war against Germany was that the United States should not attempt to resolve what essentially were conflicts between other nations. Isolationist strength reached its peak between the two wars, when Robert LaFollette, Sr., ran for president on a third-party label in 1924. Although LaFollette carried only his home state of Wisconsin, he ran a close second in several Midwestern states and compiled what was then the second largest number of votes a third-party candidate had ever received for president. The strength of the LaFollette movement raised serious questions about American entry into World War II before Pearl Harbor. However, the contrast between the Jewish groups, on the one hand, and the Irish, Italian, and German groups, on the other, is basically the same as that between the Committee of One Million and SANE. Each of the three latter groups was considerably more numerous (and remains so) than the Jewish group. Thus, the potential for these groups to swing votes was greater. Why did they fail where the Jewish groups seem to have succeeded? The answer seems to lie in the fact that the Irish, Italian, and German groups all opposed the policies of the government, while the official government position toward Israel was one of support. It therefore does not seem reasonable to argue that even a powerful ethnic group can reverse the course of foreign policy. At best, it can create a dialogue and expedite action on a policy that has a general consensus among decision-makers.

These views of the relative weakness of interest groups on security issues stand in distinct contrast to the claims that a "military-industrial" complex dominates the domestic and strategic aspects of foreign policy decision-making and that "economic imperialism" is the major motive of an unholy alliance between big business and the government on issues that affect American relations with other nations.[35] In support of the "military-industrial complex" argument, one can cite the case of Lockheed Aircraft, which appealed to the federal government in 1971 for backing of a huge loan to prevent the company from going out of business. Since Lockheed was the nation's largest defense contractor and its demise would mean that the Pentagon might not receive weapons it had already paid for, the pressures for government support became immense. Among the supporters of the loan were Senators Alan Cranston and John V. Tunney, both California Democrats, and Senators Henry Jackson and Warren Magnuson, Washington Democrats. Lockheed was a major employer in both states. Yet the Lockheed case as a prime example of a "military-industrial complex" does not make a very persuasive case. The Senate vote on the loan passed by only one vote. Jackson and Magnuson had not only supported the Lockheed loan, but were widely known as consistent supporters of increased military spending, whether the projects involved aided their constituents or not. On the other hand, Cranston and Tunney have sided against high defense budgets on Senate votes other than Lockheed. And Senator Barry Goldwater, one of the most consistent supporters of the military in Congress, voted against the Lockheed loan precisely because he believed that the federal government had no business saving a contractor that had created its own financial woes. Stated very simply, there is just no apparent pattern of support for increased defense spending or *across* specific projects to suggest that there is a unified "military-industrial complex." There may indeed be "mini-complexes," composed of a branch of the service and some contractors. However, these "mini-complexes" are more likely to oppose than to support each other. We do not assert that all members of Congress or the executive branch make decisions on foreign *or* domestic policy on the basis of the merits of the case alone. One can point too easily to members who have profited from their positions; in 1976 the House Ethics committee reprimanded Rep. Robert Sikes (D., Fla.) for improprieties in his role as chairman of the Appropriations subcommittee which dealt with military construction. (In 1977 the full Democratic caucus in the House removed Sikes from his chairmanship.) There are many other stories which are much worse than this one. However, we do maintain that there has been considerably less dishonesty than many critics of the "Washington establishment" maintain. No one has documented widespread misdeeds among either Congressmen or bureaucrats, and one suspects that those members of Congress who voted for the Lockheed loan were more embarrassed than the vast majority of Americans when they learned that these funds had partly been used to bribe foreign governments.

An argument for the "economic imperialism" thesis can similarly be made by example.[36] The attempt by the International Telephone and Telegraph Company to rig the 1970 election for president of Chile against the Socialist Salvadore Allende to protect its financial interests there is a case in point. While Nixon and Kissinger specifically rejected a plan that would have entailed the cooperation of the White House in what proved to be an unsuccessful attempt to prevent Allende from becoming president, in 1973 the CIA "destabilized" the Allende government. While there is no direct evidence that multinational corporations were also involved in the 1973 incident, Nixon did know about the CIA involvement. Thus, even if there was no firm conspiracy between business and the government, in this instance, at least, American foreign and economic policies certainly coincided. Yet, instances such as this do not establish that economic imperialism is the dominant method of conducting foreign policy.

Indeed, the United States has accepted the expropriations of American-owned property in many countries when compensation has been made to the companies involved, and it has not reneged on its support of Israel despite its dependence upon Arab oil. Relations with the Arab nations did improve markedly in recent years, but this has been viewed by both sides as a useful way of reaching a possible Middle East peace settlement through an intermediary trusted by both the Israelis and the Arabs. Despite extensive advertising campaigns by several major oil companies, the United States has not moved toward a position of nonalignment in the Middle East. Indeed, it might well be said that if the theory of imperialism had any validity, U.S. policy toward the area would have been pro-Arab from the beginning; obviously, the allegedly powerful oil companies did not dictate U.S. foreign policy. Similarly, it might be argued that Saudi Arabia, with its enormous influx of billions of dollars from oil sales, will soon turn the United States, Europe, and Japan into its colonies. The dubiousness of this assertion reflects further on the lack of persuasiveness of the idea of economic imperialism and the stranglehold large U.S. companies are supposed to have on a counterrevolutionary *security* policy. But where were the Marines when OPEC quadrupled the price of oil and dislocated and badly hurt—and continues to hurt—all Western economies? Such meekness hardly seems characteristic of the stern stuff that U.S. imperialism is supposed to be made of. In his study of the State Department's contacts with interest groups and the public, Bernard Cohen found that economic interest groups may obtain what they want if these *demands do not conflict with preestablished departmental policies.* [37] An economic interest group may indeed benefit from a foreign policy decision, but this implies nothing about whether that group actually played any role in the formulation of the decision. Perhaps the best example of this is the economic boon that some farmers and grain speculators reaped from the decision of the United States to make major wheat sales to the Soviet Union and China, without having initiated or lobbied for the deals.

The actors in the third circle of decision-making on foreign or security policy as distinct from "intermestic" policy do indeed seem relatively weak in comparison to those in the innermost circle and in the second circle. Political parties have not played a dominant role in the foreign policy debate, and this, in turn, has probably reduced the effectiveness of the congressional role in decision-making. The patterns of congressional support and opposition to foreign policy decisions of the president have not been clear-cut. A bipartisan foreign policy aids the executive branch in its battle with Congress since the president can build a new coalition of his own on each foreign policy roll call. On general domestic policies, the limits of presidential discretion are set by what the majority party in Congress will or will not accept. Interest groups appear not to have filled in the void in the power vacuum between the president and Congress. In only one area of foreign policy decision-making, the defense budget, has Congress been able to assert itself. Even if a new bipartisan or partisan opposition to presidential domination of the foreign policy decision-making process is developing on Capitol Hill, the members of Congress must still find some way to make their decisions binding upon the president. In situations in which the president is called upon to take action quickly, Congress may find developing that capacity even more difficult.

THE OUTERMOST CIRCLE: PUBLIC OPINION AND THE MEDIA

Public opinion and the media stand at the periphery of the foreign policy decision-making process. Public opinion tends to be permissive and supportive of presidential decisions in foreign policy. Indeed, the level of public support for the president, as measured by polls, increases dramatically in a foreign policy crisis—whether the resolution of the crisis is favorable to the American position or not![38] Furthermore, public opinion is not always marked by consistency: Polls may indicate that a large percentage of the American people consider a specific policy decision to be a mistake but nevertheless will support a presidential decision with which it disagrees. Critics of the policy can cite the first set of poll results, the administration the second. Each is partially correct, but the net result of the confusion is that the president can cite public support for his actions and use the power of his office to continue pursuing his chosen policies. Our discussion of public opinion will begin with a consideration of the broad limiting role of public viewpoints—of when public opinion is weak, when it becomes stronger, and the forces pushing it in various directions. We shall then consider the role of public opinion in a somewhat different context—the ways in which public opinion might be translated into policy decisions.

Support of and Opposition to the President and His Policies

The role of public opinion in foreign policy is, as we have noted, permissive and supportive of presidential discretion. The principal reason is that the vast majority of Americans are poorly informed about and uninterested in foreign policy. Most foreign policy issues are simply too far removed from their everyday frames of reference. A voter, who may be a worker, a farmer, a businessman, or a professor, will have (or will believe that he has) a certain degree of knowledge and familiarity in dealing with issues related to his sphere of livelihood (e.g., unemployment and job security or farm price subsidies), and he is also likely to hold views on various topics that relate to him as a citizen, father, and so forth (open housing, equal job opportunity, police protection, drugs, the quality and cost of medical care and education). On domestic policies he will therefore be more likely to hold his own views, even if they should differ from those of the president. On foreign policy issues, however, most voters do not have the knowledge, frame of reference, or sense of personal competence they do with affairs that are less remote.[39] This lack of factual content and intellectual structure of public opinion means that the mass public reacts to foreign policy issues in terms of moods and seeks guidance from the president.

> The general public looks for *cues* and *responses* in public discussions of foreign policy. It does not listen to the content of discussion but to its tone. A presidential statement that a crisis exists

will ordinarily be registered in the form of apprehension. A reassuring statement will be received with complacency reactions. In both cases, the reaction has no depth and no structure.[40]

Two things should be clear. First, it is the president to whom the public looks for information and interpretation of the outside world and how it affects American security interests. This means that he has considerable freedom to set his direction and mold public opinion. Second, public opinion does not usually guide the president; it is more frequently formed as a response to presidential action, not only because of public ignorance but because in foreign policy presidents frequently have to act *before* any firm public opinion has been formed. Gabriel Almond found two factors of particular importance in attracting and reducing public attention to foreign policy: "(1) the extreme dependence of public interest in foreign affairs on dramatic and overtly threatening events; (2) the extraordinary pull of domestic and private affairs even in periods of international crisis."[41] Perhaps the best way of summing up the role of public opinion in foreign policy is to emphasize its followership.

Since the Truman Doctrine in 1947, public opinion has been responsive to presidential leadership and, therefore, has been as rigid or flexible as presidential policy. It has supported hardline anti-Soviet and anti-Chinese policies when they were official policy (as they were from Truman's day right through to Johnson), and it has supported moves toward a relaxation of tensions and negotiating conflicts of interests (as during the Nixon era). Both kinds of moves received widespread popular acclaim. The public looked to the president for its cues. In a crisis this phenomenon is particularly noticeable; the public rallies around the president even if the crisis was bungled by the president, as Kennedy did the ill-fated refugee invasion of Cuba in 1961. During the opening periods of the two limited wars in which the United States has become engaged since World War II, the initial commitments received very high levels of public and congressional support, and they stayed high despite great costs, including high casualty rates, during the opening phase of the war. The fact that presidential action is prerequisite to the formation of public opinion on foreign policy issues was especially clear during the Vietnam War. There was little in the way of any opinion—either for or against—during the Kennedy Administration's incremental commitment of advisers, or even after the Gulf of Tonkin. Extensive public awareness of Vietnam came only with the sudden, visible commitment of more than 500,000 men. But perhaps a more astounding example of public opinion's followership role and inconsistency occurred with President Nixon's decision to send American troops into Cambodia. Just prior to the decision, only 7 percent of the respondents favored such a move; after the move 50 percent approved! Ford's approval rating jumped 11 percent immediately after the *Mayaguez* incident. Indeed, the public is so predisposed to view the foreign policy postures of chief executives positively that a July, 1974 Gallup poll found 54 percent of the respondents approving of how Nixon handled foreign policy. The president, who was to resign within a month in the midst of the Watergate scandal, had an overall approval rating of only 26 percent favorable responses.

Yet, while permissive and supportive, public support is not unlimited.[42] If a president's policies are not successful, if they fail to achieve their objectives in a reasonable amount of time and at a tolerable cost, the public reserves the right to punish the president and his party at election time. A Marshall Plan for the economic recovery of Western Europe, while sizable in scale, received large-scale support: It had a time limit of four years and was not particularly burdensome for the taxpayer, and the result of a rebuilt and reinvigorated Europe was highly visible. In contrast, foreign aid programs for developing areas have always been relatively unpopular. The aid seems to be unending and it clearly wins little overtly expressed goodwill for the United States. Nor does it stimulate fairly rapid modernization to the point where economic progress becomes increasingly self-sustaining. Since forecasts predict an increasing gap between the rich industrialized Western countries and the poor, essentially rural non-Western countries, the future seems to hold only a continuous, almost external aid program with no promise of quick success and relief from this capital transfer effort.

Military interventions follow the same pattern. When the president first announces an intervention the public—and Congress—will support him. Indeed, this recurrent phenomenon has led John Mueller to suggest that as long as presidents can commit troops, proposals that wars can be avoided if Congress were required to vote its approval are unlikely to work, for once the commitment has been made the tendency will be to "rally around the flag."[43] An intervention such as the Dominican intervention in 1965 may be widely criticized by foreign policy experts in and out of government, congressmen, and journalists, but if it is brought to a successful conclusion, or at least what appears to be a successful conclusion, relatively quickly, the president will suffer no electoral reprisals. On the other hand, popular support for a Korean or Vietnamese war will decline over time if the price appears to be disproportionate to the objectives sought.

Public and congressional support for the conduct of the war does not decrease significantly, despite high casualties and/or taxes, while the general belief in a reasonably short war and success on the battlefield remains prevalent. Conversely, this support erodes as hostilities drag on and the continued high costs of the conflict appear increasingly pointless as the expectation of victory disappears. In Korea, Chinese entry into the war led to a major drop of support for Truman five months after the American intervention; in Vietnam, the drop took longer, starting in the spring of 1965 and reaching a low point in late 1967, which, after a brief upsurge, was reconfirmed by the Communist Tet offensive in early 1968.[44] Even President Johnson, a skillful manipulator, could not hold off the cost of the war forever; he had postponed this cost by not drafting most American middle- and upper-class males, mainly students; not calling up the reserves; and postponing a war surcharge tax. But the support eroded, and Tet was the final proof that victory was no nearer than before and that the high costs of the war were fruitless.

Thus, in limited wars, public opinion does become relevant. Support for the wars in Vietnam and Korea declined as the costs, especially the casualty rates, increased over time. The impact of the casualty rate on the level of opposition to the war was considerably stronger for the Vietnam conflict than for

Korea.[45] That may be an indication that the nightly exposure of Vietnam casualties by the television networks had a considerable effect on the increase in opposition to the war. In both the Vietnamese and the Korean cases, the evaporation of presidential support permits other sources of information to gain a public following.

The two principal alternative sources are congressional hearings and the media. Lacking the power to change the president's Vietnam policies, Senator Fulbright used the mechanism of his Foreign Relations Committee hearings to dramatize opposition to the war. At times, the major television networks would carry live coverage of these hearings. At a minimum, the hearings would be covered on the evening network news programs and in the major newspapers across the country. The influence of such hearings—which are often long and tedious and may not bring out any new information—may be slight, but it is often almost all that opponents of a policy have in their attempt to affect public opinion. With the growth of the medium of television, the roles of the congressional committee hearings and the media have become ever more closely intertwined. Television gives opponents of a policy a more direct line to the public than did newspapers or radio—it provides for visual contact as well as the reporting of events. However, the gains that opponents of a policy have made through this newest medium have also accrued to the president. Indeed, the chief executive can always obtain free network time for an address to the nation, and he can use such speeches to rally public opinion behind his policies. On balance, the advent of television probably has meant more to opponents of a president's policy than to the chief executive himself. Since public opinion is generally permissive and supportive of presidential initiatives, any gain in exposure of the opposition's point of view may well enhance the opponents' strength. A president simply needs less exposure to rally support for his position than does the opposition.

The media are more than just devices for presenting alternative views of public officials to the mass public or, in turn, representing the mass public to the foreign policy establishment. The media also have their own impact on public opinion. Although most voters are not terribly concerned with foreign policy issues, the nightly television coverage of events in Vietnam brought an overseas war into millions of American homes each night. Furthermore, the media have not always presented presidential decisions in a favorable light. Virtually every president of the United States in recent years has believed that the press was hostile to him, "out to get him." Indeed, the Nixon Administration brought its hostilities toward the media—the television networks and national news magazines as well as the newspapers—out into the open. Johnson was less hostile to the press but did criticize several reporters and nationally syndicated columnists for their opposition to his Vietnam policies. Johnson once had occasion to query Senator Church about the senator's antiwar position at a White House reception. The president asked the senator where he was getting his information on the war effort. Church replied that his information came from the columns of the noted journalist Walter Lippmann. The president reportedly replied, "Well, the next time you want a dam in Idaho, ask Walter Lippmann for it."

Yet, even when public opinion has been mobilized—by the media, the congressional critics, or just by sheer uneasiness over the course of a foreign policy—its role still remains rather limited. The problem is that the public does not always speak with one voice. Sixty-four percent of a November, 1965, sample of Americans did *not* think that American involvement in Vietnam was a mistake, as compared to 21 percent who believed that it was. By October, 1967, the balance had shifted to the position that the war was a mistake (44 percent in favor, 46 percent opposed to the initial involvement). By the summer of 1968, a sizable majority took the position that the war was a mistake.[46] Yet the pattern of support for proposals to end the war—including both a stepped-up military posture and total withdrawal—had not changed accordingly from 1965 to 1968. Mueller has thus argued that, at any given time, "support should be considered a chord rather than a note."[47] The president can use this pattern of inconsistency among the voters to indicate that there is not enough support for any other alternative policy to warrant a shift in his position. If the lack of consistency in public opinion polls does not provide the president with a distinct message on how to choose foreign policy alternatives, might not the electoral arena? It is to this facet of public opinion's impact on foreign policy—and to the linkage between public opinion and congressional opinion—that we now turn.

Popular Control of Foreign Policy

Public opinion, according to many theorists of democratic government, does not serve as a guide to policy-makers who must choose among alternative courses of action every day. Rather, at election time the citizenry is called upon to choose its leaders and then to let those leaders determine policy choices until the next election. The electoral mechanism thus gives the voter what has been called "popular control of government." The voter, according to this thesis, does not instruct the men and women he chooses at the ballot box on what policies to adopt. Rather, he selects a candidate who represents policy positions closest to his own. This is the electoral function of public opinion.[48] An even stronger demand upon public opinion is made by other democratic theorists: that public opinion should be "converted" into public policy by the representative system of government. These theorists expect a member of Congress to represent—or, "re-present"—the views of his constituency in his voting behavior in Congress. How well the public's viewpoints are translated into policy decisions of their representatives gives us an idea of how well the democratic political system is working. This "conversion" function of public opinion demands more than the electoral function. The latter merely assumes that the voter can replace an office-holder whose views he does not like at the next election. The conversion function assumes that it is the task of the office-holder to represent faithfully the majority position in his constituency between elections as well.[49] In this section, we shall examine both views of the function of public opinion.

The concept of the electoral system as a choice between two competing sets of policy choices does indeed seem to hold true for the 1952 election. The evidence is rather straightforward that Truman's decline in popularity and the subsequent Republican victory in 1952 can be atrributed to the public's adverse reaction to the Korean War.[50] In general, however, there

appears to be no great amount of policy voting on either domestic or foreign policy issues. On the one hand, the two parties have not always offered the voter a clear-cut choice on
policy alternatives. On the other hand, there is even less evidence that voters are aware of whatever differences there may
be between two candidates for an office.

Since voters tend to be less interested in questions of foreign
policy than in domestic policies, it is not surprising to find that
policy voting on foreign affairs questions is rather rare. A study
of voters in the 1956 and 1960 presidential elections led Warren E. Miller to conclude that, at an absolute maximum, the
net contribution of the parties' foreign policy stands toward
changes in voting behavior from one election to the next was
one-half of 1 percent.[51] In an election as close as the 1960
contest, this margin may be substantial. When looked at by
itself, however, the effect of policy stands on voting is negligi-
ble. A Roper poll reported that in the 1976 elections, voters
saw domestic issues as more important in their voting decisions
than foreign policy issues by a margin of more than 12 to 1. The
results for foreign policy of more recent studies are no more
heartening for the advocate of a political system that converts
public opinion on foreign policy into public policy through
elections. A study by Gerald M. Pomper found that, from 1956
to 1972, voter attitudes and partisan affiliation became more
strongly associated in five areas of domestic policy but did not
change for the one foreign policy measure (foreign aid) he
examined.[52] There remained in 1972, as there had been in
1956, 1960, 1964, and 1968, virtually no relationship between
public opinion and party identification on this foreign policy
measure.

If the parties do not take divergent policy stands on issues,
then the voter has no way of holding either party responsible
for the decisions that are actually reached. And, since the party
label of a candidate is the easiest way a voter can separate him
from his opponent, this lack of consistency on foreign policy
positions offers little hope that the effects of public opinion will
be felt through the ballot box. There is some evidence of a
relationship between general dissatisfaction with Johnson's
performance as president and anti-Democratic votes in
1968.[53] However, there was virtually no policy voting on the

Vietnam issue in that election: The patterns of support for
Humphrey and Nixon were almost totally unrelated to the
voters' positions on Vietnam.[54] The reason, however, was not
that the voters were not polarized on Vietnam. Rather 57
percent of the sample saw either no difference or very little
difference in the Vietnam planks of the two candidates![55] In
fact, Nixon appeared to do slightly better among advocates of
pulling soldiers out of Vietnam than did Humphrey,[56] and
considerably better among advocates of a stronger military
posture. Indeed, the evidence is mixed as to whether there was
any relationship at all between Johnson's popularity and the
increasing opposition to the war in Vietnam.[57]

If there is little support for the concept of popular control
of governmental policy through the electoral arena, then we
should not expect a much stronger linkage between the public
and their representatives in Congress. If this is the case, then
the democratic dilemma becomes even more pronounced. If
Congress finds the means to reassert itself on foreign policy but
is acting otherwise than its constituents want it to, what does
this mean for foreign policy under a democratic government?
The very idea behind the conversion process is that public
opinion is translated into public policy through the actions of
the representatives in the legislature. To do so, members of
Congress must of course know the views of their constituents.

In studies of the influence of constituency views upon the
attitudes and behavior of members of the House, Warren E.
Miller and Donald E. Stokes found that the conversion process
works quite well on civil rights, moderately well on social welfare issues, and virtually not at all on foreign policy questions.
On civil rights questions in particular, the views of constituents
were in general consistent with the representatives' roll call
votes.[58] If we assume that a congressman might not always be
able to identify the feelings of his constituents and instead
bases his voting behavior on what he *believes* his constituents
think, then the conversion process on civil rights roll calls is
extremely strong. This is not surprising, since civil rights questions are redistributive issues: Both the representative and his
constituents perceive "winners" and "losers" domestically,
and it is reasonable to suppose that they identify the same
groups as "winners" and the same groups as "losers."

For foreign policy votes, on the other hand, there is at least a weak tendency for members of the House to take stands different from those espoused by their constituents. When representatives' perceptions of constituency attitudes are employed instead of simple constituency attitudes, only a moderately positive relationship between perceptions and votes is noticeable. The upshot is that most representatives do not have a very good idea of what their constituents want. The linkage between actual and perceived constituency attitudes is more than three times as great for civil rights bills as it is for foreign policy roll calls. And, finally, the personal attitudes of representatives show virtually no relationship to constituency attitudes on foreign policy votes.[59] It is thus hardly surprising that Richard F. Fenno found that members of the House International Relations committee saw their service on that body as not particularly helpful to their reelection efforts, in contrast to membership on such committees as Interior and Post Office.[60]

These results suggest that measures designed to strengthen the role of Congress in the foreign policy process will not necessarily bring foreign policy more in line with public opinion. If anything, public opinion seems to follow presidential opinion more than it does congressional opinion. Even when guided by opinion leaders in opposition to the president, the public tends to be more responsive to the chief executive. Yet, when opinions do become divided on a policy area, such as the war in Vietnam, the failure of the party system to play the role of opinion leader serves as a strong check on the conversion of public preferences into public policy in the foreign policy arena.

Still, a president cannot forget public opinion before he makes decisions; he is indeed very conscious of it, as it affects his desire to be reelected or for his party's candidate to win, and he is therefore quite aware of what might happen if the citizen-consumer does not like his policy-products. (Carl Friedrich has called this "the law of anticipated reaction.") Before World War II, the isolationist consensus set the constraints within which foreign policy decisions had to be made. Even joining the International Court of Justice became impossible; Roosevelt's call in 1937 for the democracies to "quarantine" the aggressors met with a public furor. After World War II, Truman did not oppose the rapid demobilization of the armed forces despite increasing tensions with the Soviet Union. The public wanted to relax, to bring boys back home, to concentrate once more on domestic and private affairs. Not until eighteen months after the war against Japan had ended, after the perception of repeated demonstrations of Soviet hostility and numerous vetoes in the United Nations, did the Soviet threat appear sufficiently clear that Truman felt he could go before Congress and the public and ask them to support the policy of containment. And the reaction to Vietnam and our frequently criticized role as world policeman suggests that U.S. policy in the post-Vietnam period will have to assume a "lower profile" if it is to retain public—and congressional—support.

The four circles of power we have proposed do seem to indicate the relative impact of each set of actors on the foreign policy process. The president, because he can listen to whom he wishes, and because he can generally command the support of the public (and Congress as well), stands at the center of the decision-making process. Surrounding him are key personal advisers and the leaders of the major foreign policy agencies in the government. These leaders in turn depend upon the actors immediately below them in their respective departments for detailed advice and recommendations, which they carry into the innermost circle.

Standing at somewhat greater distance from the center of power are Congress, the political parties, and interest groups. While each may attempt to perform some role in decision-making, their successes are far outnumbered by those of the president. Congress has asserted itself on the defense budget and has been trying to take on a greater role on broader foreign policy questions, but it has yet to find the mechanism to obtain more power. Congress and the media may try to lead the voters, but the voters do not seem to follow. Their positions are often poorly articulated, and even when they become clearer there is no guarantee that anyone in a position of authority will be there to listen. The dilemma the average voter faces also affects Congress in its role as an opinion leader: It is well expressed by John Dewey in a 1926 statement that "the Public seems to be lost; it is certainly bewildered."[61]

MODELS OF POLICY-MAKING

How do the various actors who participate in foreign policy-making interact? To examine this question, two models of the policy-making process will be presented. The first model we shall examine is the *rational actor* approach; the second is the *bureaucratic.* These models are devices by which we, as outside observers and analysts, organize our perceptions about how decisions are made. We do not assume that the various actors necessarily "choose" one model or the other and then make their decisions on the basis of that model. Rather, we describe possible methods of decision-making when we posit the models. We will then examine several specific foreign policy decisions in light of these models.

The rational actor model assumes that decision-makers will (1) select the objectives and values that a given policy is supposed to achieve and maximize; (2) consider the various alternative means to achieve these purposes; (3) calculate the likely consequences of each alternative course; and (4) choose the course most likely to attain the objectives originally selected. The government is often viewed as a unitary actor when the rational actor model is used. This is implicit in the phrases we use or read: "The United States has decided . . . ," "It is believed that Moscow seeks . . . ," and "China has announced. . . ."

Decision-makers have goals and attempt to maximize them in the policy-making arena. Deterrence of nuclear war, for

example, assumes that a potential aggressor will not attack if
the price of destroying his adversary is far higher than any
conceivable gains he might make.[1] Nuclear devastation is
clearly a price totally disproportionate to any possible profit.
Deterrence thus rests upon the assumption that the party to
be deterred is rational and that he will reject alternative
courses of action—that is, he will not attack and commit sui-
cide or choose a third course such as refusing to defend his own
interests and withdrawing into isolationism. Or, consider the
rationale for limited war. In 1957, Henry A. Kissinger published a book, *Nuclear Weapons and Foreign Policy,* in which
he argued that since the United States's strategy of massive
retaliation gave the president only two options—deterrence
or, if challenged, fighting a total war—America's adversary
(then still perceived as a united Sino-Soviet bloc) would be able
to confront him with limited challenges in areas of vital interest to the United States.[2] This would then put Washington up
against a dilemma: Either respond completely and risk nuclear
immolation, or don't respond and appease or yield. The rational alternative in these circumstances was to have a limited
war capability to respond to such less than total challenges.

This assumption of rationality, it should be added, is not
confined to the study of international politics and foreign policy. It is, for example, the basis of the free market economy
with its assumption that man seeks to maximize profits. And,
in the area of domestic politics in the United States, it has been
used to study the behavior of political parties on specific issues:
Here we assume that in the electoral market place, as in the
economic one, the consumer chooses, among the alternative
policies offered, the one most likely to satisfy his preferences.[3]
The rational actor model has been dominant in explaining
international politics—to a far greater degree than in domestic
politics.[4] Because most decisions studied in international politics have involved relations among nations, students of international politics have tended to view nations as unitary actors. In
crisis decision-making, this assumption is particularly reasonable. In a crisis, the scope of the decision-making arena is
rather small. The inner circle makes the decisions and is almost
invariably supported by Congress, the bureaucracies, and public opinion. It is not necessary to assume, however, that an

entire nation—and only an entire nation—can be thought of as a unitary actor under the rational model. On the one hand, several nations forming an alliance can be considered a unitary actor. On the other hand, we may find subnational coalitions within a country. Conflict over redistributing income from the "haves" to the "have nots" is, for example, a good domestic illustration of two coalitions of rational actors opposing each other. Similarly, opposing subnational coalitions, as we shall see, may be in conflict over a foreign policy issue. The basic trouble with the rational actor model is that there is no room for compromise. One side—a nation, a coalition of nations, or subnational groups—will win, and the other will lose, because there is only one "best" policy.

The second model, the bureaucratic, sees the government as composed of many actors, encompassing all four circles of power, but focusing on the president and the bureaucracy. Actors in different organizational settings—the Departments of State and Defense, Congress, or, even more specifically, the European desk in State *vs.* the African desk, the Air Force *vs.* the Navy, the Senate Foreign Relations Committee *vs.* the Senate Armed Services Committee—approach a problem from different perspectives. Indeed, each is likely to see a different part or "face" of the same problem. Policy-making in these circumstances involves attempts to reconcile the policy preferences of the various "players" with their different perceptions and interests. The issue is not whose policy position and recommendations are correct, but how to reconcile conflicting views of what the correct policy ought to be. We again assume that actors have values that they wish to maximize, but we also accept the idea that each actor is willing to settle for only a part of his goals and compromise on the rest rather than get nothing at all. Compromise is the hallmark of this model, and it is not difficult to see why this approach, rather than the rational actor one, has dominated explanations of domestic politics.[5]

The process by which different proposals are compromised or "aggregated" into a single policy decision or "output" has been called "partisan mutual adjustment."[6] "Partisan" does not in this context refer to political parties. Rather, the different actors in a decision-making situation are "partisans" in the sense that they will each articulate and pursue their own positions. The process of "mutual adjustment" among partisans suggests that some form of bargaining takes place among the interested parties. No single partisan group is strong enough to impose its position on the other groups involved. As Charles E. Lindblom has argued, "There is no highest prescriptive authoirty in government: no agency, legislator, executive, or continuing collectivity of legislators can prescribe to all others yet concede no authority to any other."[7] Bureaucratic politics is therefore characterized on the one hand by conflicts of interests and viewpoints and on the other hand by bargaining and compromises. Perhaps the best example of this in domestic politics occurs in the budgetary process. The total budget cannot equal merely the sum of all budget requests from federal agencies: If the government were to try this approach, it would go broke very quickly. On the other hand, no agency can be denied funding altogether. Therefore, in the budgetary process each agency makes its demands and is willing to settle for a lesser amount.

An example of the use of these two different models and how they produced different conclusions may be found in analyzing Soviet foreign policy and the American-Soviet balance of power during the late 1950s. The American government at that time became extremely worried about a possible "missle gap" favorable to the Soviets. Using the rational actor approach, it seemed justifiable to assume that, having been the first to test an ICBM, Moscow would exploit this technological breakthrough by attempting large-scale production and would use the ICBM deployment politically to effect major political changes, particularly in Western Europe, where the Kremlin was seeking to drive the Americans out of West Berlin. Khrushchev did in fact talk of mass-producing the missiles, and American intelligence worriedly forecast a missile gap on the basis of Soviet industrial capacity.

Had the American government considered the situation in terms of the bureaucratic model, it might have been more wary. Immediate, massive Soviet deployment of ICBMs was unlikely because strategic rockets (as the Russians called them) were controlled by the Soviet Army, which was not very interested in ICBMs. Additionally, ICBM development and deployment would have required a large shift of funds from other military requirements, and this would have created noisy quarrels among the competing services. Thus, the use of different models in analyzing an adversary's behavior had quite different implications for American foreign and defense policies.[8] The incoming Kennedy Administration, acting on conclusions drawn from the rational model, initiated a sizable American missile buildup. This led the Russians to react to their humiliation in the Cuban missile crisis of 1962 by increasing still further the size of their own ICBM capability.

In explaining the foreign policy decisions of the United States, we suggest that the rational actor model is more relevant to crisis decisions, whereas the bureaucratic model applies best to explaining program policies such as the defense budget or foreign aid. These program policies require cooperation of many different actors, especially Congress, because they need annual funding. Crisis decisions, on the other hand, cannot wait for an internal consensus among the various governmental actors to "emerge." Indeed, they require immediate action, the type of action best taken by a president plus a small number of top-level advisers. Given the fact that they all perceive themselves to be engaged in an emergency, they tend to subordinate conflicting bureaucratic interests and positions to the need for a rapid decision.

Under the Nixon Administration, however, both crisis decisions and program decisions followed the rational actor model. All decisions—indeed, even domestic ones—were justified by the administration on the ground that the alternative selected maximized a clearly delineated goal that the administration had posted. Nixon disliked the politics of bargaining and compromises, believing that it did not produce sound policy; that is, policy would tend to be the product of the dynamics of the policy-making process rather than a rational response to the external problem confronting the nation.[9] Thus, he attempted to centralize decision-making in the White House rather than in the bureaucracy. This was particularly the case on foreign policy questions. Often the decision-making circle consisted of only himself, Kissinger, and one or two other close advisers. Nixon, far more than his predecessors, asserted the primacy of the presidency. Often, the attempt to centralize decision-mak-

ing in the White House was resisted by other actors in the
foreign policy-making process, producing a situation of opposing subnational coalitions, each attempting to attain its goals.
We shall see such a situation in the decision to deploy an
antiballistic missile (ABM) system in the Nixon Administration
and shall contrast this style of decision-making to an earlier
ABM decision under Johnson.

THE RATIONAL ACTOR MODEL AND CRISIS DECISIONS: THE CUBAN MISSILE CRISIS AND THE MINING OF HAIPHONG HARBOR

Crises, as we have seen, are characterized by a number of
features: a perceived threat to vital interests, usually surprise,
and sense of urgency to make decisions.[10] Overhanging the
situation, in which one state has confronted another with a
demand for a change in the status quo, is the possible use of
violence, possibly a nuclear war. One characteristic of the decision-making process is, therefore, that the decisions will be
made at the very top of the governmental hierarchy by the
president and his closest advisers. Some will be his statutory
advisers, such as the secretaries of his chief foreign policy agencies, others men both in and out of government whose judgment the president particularly trusts. Thus, during the
potentially very explosive Cuban missile crisis of 1962,[11] which
occurred after the Russians had sent approximately seventy
intermediate and medium-range missiles to the island, the Executive Committee, which managed the cirsis, listed as its
members the president and vice-president, the secretaries of
state and defense; their seconds in command; the director of
the CIA; the chairman of the Joint Chiefs of Staff; the president's special assistant for National Security Affairs; the secretary of the treasury; the Attorney General (the president's
brother); his special counsel (perhaps the president's closest
friend among his advisers); an ambassador just returned from
Moscow; and President Truman's former secretary of state.
But during the 1972 crisis following the spring offensive of
North Vietnamese troops across the demilitarized zone sepa-
rating North and South Vietnam—where the offensive had not

been expected—when the defeat of the South Vietnamese armies seemed imminent, the decision-making process was even more narrowly confined. Partly as a result of the concentration of foreign policy decision-making in the White House under Henry Kissinger, partly as a result of the president's style as a "loner," and partly as a result of the Nixon tactic of confronting a Senate increasingly critical of the continuation of the Vietnam War with faits accomplis (which could not be done if leaks occurred), the decision-making seems to have been confined largely to the two men.[12]

A second characteristic of crisis decisions is the central role of the president; it is he who, more than anyone else, interprets events and evaluates the stakes in the crisis. Kennedy's and Nixon's "readings" of the nature of the situations they confronted, the consequences these situations might have upon U.S. security and their own political futures and ability to lead the nation, were responsible for their actions. (The latter two considerations can hardly be separated, for the external challenges, as presidents see them, do not really leave them with a choice of accepting a personal loss of prestige without accepting as well a loss of national prestige. For a president of the United States, personal and national cost calculations tend to become identical.) Kennedy saw the installation of Soviet missiles in Cuba as a personal challenge with damaging national effects. In response to earlier congressional and public clamor about possible offensive missiles in Cuba—as distinct from surface-to-air defensive missiles—Kennedy had publicly declared that the United States would not tolerate offensive missiles on the island ninety miles off the Florida coast. Intended primarily as a declaration to cool American domestic criticism, which had come largely from Republicans, Kennedy's statement had also led Moscow to respond that it had no intention of placing missiles in Cuba; Russia had more than enough missiles at home. Thus the president had initially deemphasized the possibility that the Russians would install such weapons in Cuba, and Moscow had then signaled it understood Kennedy's declaration; in private, it had further reassured him that it had no intentions of installing missiles anywhere outside of the U.S.S.R.. Kennedy was thus publicly pledged to act if the Russians lied—as it turned out they had—unless he wished to be publicly humiliated. If he did not act in these circumstances, the Soviet leader, Nikita Khrushchev, would not believe other pledges and commitments the President had made or was obligated to fulfill by virtue of their existence when he had acceded to the presidency. At least, this is how the President perceived the situation.

The consequences were judged as very dangerous by Kennedy, who already feared that Khrushchev interpreted previous acts by Kennedy not as acts of restraint but as signs of a lack of will, an absence of sufficient resolution and determination on the part of the United States to defend its vital interests. During the abortive CIA-supported refugee invasion of Cuba in 1961, Kennedy had refused to commit U.S. forces once the invasion appeared doomed, although Washington had wanted to eliminate Castro. During the building of the Berlin Wall the same year, American forces had stood by as the wall went up. Khrushchev began to talk openly of America's failure of nerve. The United States apparently talked loudly but carried a small stick. Thus failure to act in the Caribbean, which has traditionally been an area within America's sphere of influence (as Eastern Europe was Russia's, and so in East Germany in 1953 and Hungary in 1956—as in Czechoslovakia in 1968—the United States kept its hands off during Russia's times of trouble), would have immense and damaging consequences. It was not so much the effect of the Soviet missiles upon the military equation between the two powers, although that was important; it was the political consequences of the *appearance* of a change in the balance of power that were deemed critical by Kennedy. The Soviet Union was supposed to be on the short end of the missile gap. But American inaction would, Kennedy feared, be widely recognized as a persuasive answer to the U.S. claims of missile superiority, would lead allied governments to fear that in the new situation, with America highly vulnerable to nuclear devastation, they could no longer count on the United States to defend them. In these circumstances the Soviets would be tempted to exploit the situation and seek to disintegrate America's alliances—especially NATO since Khrushchev had already restated his determination to eject the Western allies from West Berlin. Thus, while the risks of action in Cuba were obviously great, the risks of escalation as a result of *in*action were also perceived as great. If Khrushchev got away with Cuba, why should he take seriously Kennedy's pledge to defend West Berlin? And if he did not, would not Soviet and American troops soon be clashing in an area where they would be hard to separate?

The real irony of the Cuban missile crisis is that Kennedy was also determined that during his years in office he would try to seek a more stable and restrained basis of coexistence with the Soviet Union. This long-range goal, which hardly had the massive support it has today, could not be realized if Khrushchev would not take Kennedy seriously or felt he could push Kennedy around; then serious negotiations, recognizing each other's legitimate interests, would be impossible. Thus a major change in the cold war atmosphere was at stake, in addition to America's reputation for power and willingness to keep commitments. Domestically, of course, another "defeat" in Cuba, discrediting Kennedy's foreign policy, was bound to affect Kennedy's personal standing with his party, Congress, and the public and lead to, among other things, strong right-wing Republican pressures to be more forceful in the future and endangering the New Frontier's liberal domestic reforms.

Nixon in Vietnam also saw the central issue as America's reputation for power or its prestige.[13] When he came into office, there was little question that American opinion was weary of the high cost, especially in casualties, of the Vietnam War. The cost seemed totally disproportionate for the continuation of a war that promised no successful end in the near future. For Nixon, the crux of the problem was not whether the United States got out of Vietnam but, as he repeatedly stressed, how it got out. If America's chief adversaries, Russia and China, were to be deterred and contained, if fruitful negotiations were to occur on arms control with Moscow and relations opened up with Peking, and if a more stable "structure of peace" were to be worked out with those two capitals, then America's perceived reputation in the two major Communist countries was the crucial factor. If the United States were humiliated in Vietnam, then, regardless of whether the major U.S. commitment of its armed forces in 1965 should have been made or not, the United States would be viewed as a "pitiful, helpless giant" who could be pressured, with whom one need not negotiate seriously on a basis of the mutual recognition and acceptance of legitimate security interests, and who offered few attractions as a potential partner to either Russia or China against the other.

Nixon's strategy was, therefore, to withdraw U.S. ground forces gradually, minimize casualties, reduce the draft, and eventually end it, in order to reduce domestic opposition to the war and allow him to appeal over the heads of much of the critical sector of opinion leadership to the "silent majority," the mass public, for support of his policy of "Vietnamization." This meant that the South Vietnamese Army would increasingly take over the fighting, but it would receive large-scale U.S. air support so as to avoid a forcible takeover by Hanoi of Saigon (in other words, to preserve a non-Communist government in South Vietnam). If public opinion would support a low-cost strategy in casualties for the United States—not necessarily a low-cost strategy for the Vietnamese, North and South —if the pressure for America to get out completely could be greatly reduced at home, then Hanoi would presumably gain an incentive to negotiate a compromise settlement of the war. Confronted by the continued participation in the war of U.S. air power and—it was hoped—an increasingly well-trained South Vietnamese Army equipped by the United States, with its hopes for an all-out victory in the South dimming as the costs of the war continued to drain its strength, Hanoi would prefer to end the hostilities rather than continue fighting and would settle for political competition to gain a share of the power in Saigon.

It was this whole strategy that faced disaster in the spring of 1972, just after Nixon's dramatic visit to Peking and just before his extremely important visit to Moscow to negotiate the limitations of defensive and offensive missiles and other key topics. Nixon, like Kennedy, rejected the possibility of inaction, even though the Moscow summit meeting with its potential for dramatically changing the nature of the U.S.-Soviet adversary-partnership relationship for the better might be jeopardized if he took strong action against the Soviet Union's fraternal socialist state. But the president felt that Moscow, having supplied Hanoi with much of its modern paraphernalia of war, such as ground-to-air missiles and tanks for its current conventional offensive, should have restrained Hanoi just before the summit. As Nixon perceived the situation, whether or not Moscow was aware of the timing of Hanoi's offensive, the fact was that the offensive seriously endangered Nixon's Vietnamization policy and this would humiliate him on the eve of vital negotiations. The president did not intend to enter the negotiations under a cloud of defeat and failure. The failure of Vietnamization also would, of course, discredit the president's prestige and leadership at home. Thus Nixon, who had already ordered the bombing of North Vietnam, now ordered the additional step of mining its harbors to stop incoming Russian and Chinese supplies. Johnson had always refused to take this step; the risk of a confrontation with Moscow was too high. Did the latter not have the right to supply its friend? Would Washington have permitted Russia to blockade its supplies to South Vietnam? In any event, Nixon took the risk of a confrontation. Negotiations with Hanoi had not gotten anywhere; Vietnamization did not seem much more successful. The president, therefore, re-Americanized the war and, by risking a direct confrontation with the U.S.S.R., hoped to compel it to presure Hanoi to settle the war—if the U.S.S.R. wanted better relations with the United States. The Russians did not call off the Moscow summit meeting.

Whether Nixon considered other courses of action remains unknown. Kennedy did: everything from diplomatic pressures, a secret approach to Castro, surgical air strike on the missiles, invasion, and blockade. However, feeling strongly that he had to act in order to impress Khrushchev, Kennedy chose the blockade as the option most likely to attain the removal of the Soviet missiles. While the blockade could not by itself achieve this objective, it (1) was a sign of American determination, (2) permitted the United States the option of increasing the pressure on Moscow later if Moscow would not remove its missiles, (3) provided a relatively safe middle course between inaction and invasion or an air strike, which might provoke the Russians, and (4) placed on Khrushchev the responsibility of deciding whether to escalate or de-escalate. It is significant to note that, thanks to a U-2 "spy plane," the administration had an entire week in which to debate the meaning and significance of the Russian move, what its military and political effects were likely to be on U.S. security interests, what the different courses of actions open to the United States were, and which was most likely to achieve the removal of the Soviet missiles without precipitating nuclear war. Many crises simply do not allow such time for preparation and the careful consideration of the many alternative actions that can be undertaken. Even during the missile crisis, the initial reaction of most of the president's advisers was to bomb the missile sites. Slowing down the momentum of events becomes crucial if impulsive actions are to be avoided.

In the Vietnam situation, Nixon apparently made his decision during the week before he announced the mining—that is, after Kissinger had flown to Moscow to talk to Russia's leaders and after he had, upon the latter's urgings, met privately with Hanoi's top negotiator in Paris, to no avail. Nixon and Kissinger, and reportedly also Secretary of the Treasury Connally (but not, apparently, the secretaries of state and defense or the chairman of the Joint Chiefs), thus had less time than Kennedy in Cuba, a situation more like Truman's after the North Korean invasion of South Korea, or Kennedy's when the Berlin Wall went up, or Johnson's when the internal Dominican situation erupted and the embassy began reporting the likelihood that "Castro Communists" might gain control. In short, this was a more typical crisis.

As one might imagine, a third characteristic of crises and the accompanying sense of urgency to make a decision, as well as the perception by the policy-makers that the nation's security is at stake and the possibility of war looms so threateningly, is the subordination of bureaucratic interests to the need to make a decision to safeguard the "national interest." Crisis decision-making takes place at the top level of the government, and the men in these positions, while reflecting their departmental viewpoints, do not necessarily feel themselves limited to representing these perspectives. Organizational affiliation is not per se a good predictor of their stands.[14] McNamara did not reflect the Joint Chiefs' impulse to bomb and invade during the missile crisis (as later in Vietnam, he was increasingly to disagree with their views and recommendations); he became the leading advocate of the blockade. Other players did not even represent foreign policy bureaucracies—

the two closest men to the president, the Attorney General and the president's special counsel; the secretary of the treasury; and the ex-secretary of state, for example, represented themselves and only themselves. Thus the bureaucratic axiom that "you stand where you sit" is not necessarily correct, at least during crises.

During the Nixon Administration, indeed, the bureaucracies were subordinated to, if not bypassed by, the White House. Precisely in order to avoid as much as possible foreign policy decisions that were primarily the outcome of bureaucratic infighting and compromise rather than rational responses to the perceived external challenges and problems confronting the nation, the president decided that he and his national security assistant would determine what issues were the most important and how they would be handled. "I refuse to be confronted with a bureaucratic consensus that leaves me no options but acceptance or rejection," he said, "and that gives me no way of knowing what alternatives exist."[15] Nixon and Kissinger were assisted by a fairly sizable staff recruited by the latter. Its identification was with the president, not with different bureaucracies. This way of making decisions was applied to all foreign policy decisions, not just crisis decisions. Bureaucratic interests, while not totally eliminated, were thus greatly limited and subjected to presidential perspectives and interests.

Finally, crisis decision-making is characterized by congressional noninvolvement. Congressional leaders are usually called in and informed of the president's decision just before he announces it publicly. This is done as a matter of courtesy. But their advice is not requested. Presidents consider themselves more representative than any senator or House member and as representative as Congress as a whole. Moreover, as the term "crisis" suggests, such occurrences are perceived by one side as affecting vital interests and frequently happen suddenly and unexpectedly, leaving decision-makers with a sharp sense that they have to make rapid decisions lest the situation deteriorate further. A lack of decision time tends to mean that Congress is bound to be bypassed, except for briefings *after* decisions have been made by the executive. The president has a full-time job—indeed, burns the midnight oil—at such times just consulting his staff and cabinet officers to obtain all possible information on what is happening and interpretations as to the adversary's motives, to canvass the alternative courses of action among which he must choose, and to explore which of these is most likely to achieve his aims without triggering a nuclear exchange.

Congress may be bypassed for yet another reason. During confrontations of the superpowers, they begin by testing each other's will and determination by some "low-level" action. Thus in Cuba, Kennedy decided on the blockade as an initial move even though it could only prevent the further shipment of missiles to the island, not eliminate the ones already there. But the hope was that Moscow would perceive the blockade as a demonstration of American determination to achieve that objective; if convinced by the blockade, the Soviet Union would withdraw its missiles before Kennedy had to escalate the crisis. He could, for example, have ordered an air strike upon the missiles or an invasion, and these options remained available to him; Moscow knew that and was unwilling to risk such an escalation. In short, crises, precipitated by the attempt of one side to change the status quo and the other's equal resolution not to permit such a change, become elaborate maneuvers in which each side seeks to achieve its aim but simultaneously avoid a nuclear exchange. Thus it becomes vital first to start on one of the lower rungs of the "escalation ladder" and second to give the opponent at each higher rung sufficient time to consider risks, costs, and payoffs of either desisting, escalating, or settling the issue at stake through negotiations. These steps must be carefully timed, coordinated, and calculated, for the risks of miscalculation are ever present. It is interesting to note that the first counsel of Kennedy's advisers was to bomb the Soviet missile sites. Only after a week of deliberation did Kennedy and his advisers decide on the blockade; and normally presidents do not have a week's grace to prepare their moves but must decide virtually overnight what to do when unexpectedly they confront a major challenge.

Significantly, however, when a delegation of congressmen was called in to be told of the Russian missiles and what the United States intended to do about them, the delegation's initial reaction was skepticism as to the blockade's ability to compel the withdrawal of the missiles, and it urged an air strike (Fulbright was one of these advocates). Presumably, had Congress been consulted, given the intensely hostile mood of Congress against Castro and Cuba at that time, it would have pressed the administration to bomb or possibly invade the island, thus starting the confrontation near the top of the escalation ladder, attacking Russian installations, killing Russian personnel, and perhaps—if an invasion had occurred—overthrowing a friend and ally of Russia whom Moscow had pledged to defend. The risks of these courses, in contrast to the blockade, would have been enormous. Consulting Congress, asking for a supportive resolution, would also have robbed the Administration of the advantage of surprise and allowed the U.S.S.R. to take preemptive steps that might have made it difficult or impossible for Kennedy to act at all. In any event, it is clear that the president has much more room to maneuver if he is not subject to congressional pressures. Congress, on the whole, has not been a force for restraint—except in the later Vietnam years, when Congress climbed off the presidential bandwagon it had occupied earlier.

THE BUREAUCRATIC MODEL AND PROGRAM DECISIONS: JOHNSON AND THE ABM

In contrast to crisis decision-making, program decisions on such questions as the military budget and the development of new weapons systems typically involve a multiplicity of actors, a much longer time span in the decision-making process, and different perceptions among the actors as to what is at stake. There is a multiplicity of actors by the very nature of program policies. Such policies are developed in the bureaucracies, are sometimes of concern to interest groups (which might be helpful or hurt economically by the decision made), and are finally resolved by Congress through an appropriations bill. In the first of the specific program decisions we are considering— Johnson's decision in 1967 to proceed with the procurement of some long-term lead items on an ABM system—the actors involved included not only the president, his advisers, and other members of the inner circle such as the secretaries of defense and state and the chairman of the Joint Chiefs of Staff, but also lower-level offices in Defense, members of Congress, and (albeit, indirectly) public opinion.

Because so many actors are involved, a program decision will necessarily take more time. The defense budget, for example, is formulated in the Pentagon, reviewed by the secretary of defense, examined again by the Office of Management and Budget, sent to the authorizing committees in each house of Congress and then to the appropriating committees, and finally decided upon by members of each house. At each stage in the decision-making process, participants have the opportunity to garner support for their preferred alternatives, to engage in coalition-building in preparation for the final vote in Congress. The decision on the ABM is no exception to this general pattern. Indeed, the ABM was first proposed in the 1950s, and no concrete decision on how far development of the system would proceed was made until 1967. Upon acceding to office in 1963, Johnson attempted to forestall a decision that might antagonize either supporters or opponents of the new weapons system. Not surprisingly, the course of action he finally chose did not settle the issue once and for all.

Because each of the actors in a bureaucratic situation may, in addition, see the stakes differently, the potential for compromise is strong. However, it is not possible for any actor to impose some compromise upon the others. The various actors in the ABM decision did indeed see the stakes differently. Some were concerned with the impact that building the system would have upon the arms race, others were worried about the Soviet ICBM buildup, and at least one actor was concerned with the electoral consequences of the decision. While the various actors saw the stakes differently, there was strong disagreement as to whether the ABM would maximize the goals posited by any actor. Supporters and opponents were virtually deadlocked in 1967, and neither side was willing to concede to the other. Johnson would have preferred not to make any decision at all, to let the two sides reach some compromise. Such a strategy, as we shall argue below, was simply not available to him. Therefore, on two occasions, he took the next best step: making a "minimal decision," an action that "avoid[s] disagreement by postponing the consideration of issues over which long and determined conflicts are certain to be waged."[16] Such a decision does not resolve the issue once and for all, but leaves each side believing that it has won at least a partial victory.

Before examining the context of the 1967 decision, it will be useful to examine the historical perspective in which the decision was made. The first American ABM was the Nike-Zeus, developed in 1957 but authorized two years earlier. The Nike-Zeus was contracted by the army, with an alternative system, the Wizard, contracted by the navy. Thus, like the more general type of military appropriations decisions, the ABM battle began with interservice rivalry. The entire issue was immersed in bureaucratic conflict from its inception. Secretary of Defense Neil McElroy, worried about the launching of Sputnik by the Soviets and the Russian gain in ICBM strength, crushed the interservice rivalry in 1958 by ordering all development work on the Wizard terminated and a heavy emphasis on Nike-Zeus development. Questions about the feasibility of Nike-Zeus remained, however, and President Eisenhower decided against deployment in 1959, although recommending continued research and development. The first American success in the ABM field came in 1961, when the Nike-Zeus successfully intercepted a surface-to-air missile. The impetus for even further development of an ABM was spurred by a 1961–62 Rand study, which concluded that retaliatory strikes could not provide a defense against a Soviet first strike. In early 1963, the army proposed an expanded ABM system, the Nike-X. The Senate Armed Services Committee that year authorized $196 million for ABM parts procurement, but the Kennedy Administration opposed the plan and it went down to defeat before the full Senate.

Congressional and military pressure to deploy an ABM increased later in 1963 after the Soviets had announced that they had designed an effective ABM. The next year the Soviets paraded their ABM through Red Square in Moscow, and the Chinese announced that they had detonated their first atomic device. In the meantime, Nike-X was still in the development stage. Not until October, 1965, did the United States Army present plans for ABM deployment to the Defense Department. Johnson had continued Kennedy's opposition to the system, and McNamara refused to spend the almost $170 million Congress appropriated for ABM procurement in 1966.

The next year was the critical one for the American ABM. In January, 1967, Johnson reiterated his opposition to deployment until completion of the arms control negotiations he wanted to initiate with the Soviet Union. Nevertheless, he did include a request for procurement of an ABM system in his defense budget. Congressional supporters of the ABM were becoming less patient with Johnson's refusal to join them in support of the system and were pressuring the White House for a final decision. In the first "minimal decision," Johnson decided that including procurement funds in the defense budget was his only alternative to supporting deployment.[17] Congress acted relatively quickly on the ABM. Following the February announcement by the Soviets that they had begun to deploy an effective ABM system, the Senate voted $377 million for ABM procurements in March. House action was completed a few months later. Three votes on the ABM occurred in each house. Each Senate vote found only three members in opposition; the House votes ranged from a low of one dissenter to a maximum of only twenty-six nay votes.

The conflict was not, however, limited to the president and Congress. Indeed, Johnson was more of a neutral actor who was leaning against deployment. The strongest opposition to an ABM came from McNamara. Along with Secretary of State Rusk and the ACDA, he felt that an American decision to deploy an ABM would mean a spiraling and costly arms race that would also destroy all chances for stabilization of the American-Soviet deterrent balance. McNamara contended that an American decision to deploy the ABM would virtually preclude any possibility of initiating arms limitations talks with the Soviets. While Johnson did not agree with McNamara on the likely effects of deployment,[18] he was willing to postpone a final decision on the ABM until he had received word from the Soviets on the possibility of such talks.

McNamara was also skeptical of the feasibility of the proposed ABM. The Nike-Zeus system was rejected because of its inadequate radar facilities, and the Nike-X had been challenged on similar grounds (among others). The defense secretary, however, was in a minority position within his own department on the question of feasibility. The Pentagon's Offices of Defense Research and Engineering and Systems Analysis both supported deployment. Within Defense, only the Office of International Security Affairs joined McNamara in opposition to the ABM.

The principal supporters of the ABM were the services and key members of the Senate Armed Services Committee. In contrast to most defense budget situations, the ABM debate found the three services united in their support for a weapons system.[19] While the army, navy, and air force each "saw a different face of ABM and reached different conclusions,"[20] the very fact of this interservice agreement is worth noting. In the past, McNamara had used divisons among the services to prevail on issues of defense spending. However, the united front forced the secretary to appeal above the services directly to the president. General Earle Wheeler, chairman of the Joint Chiefs of Staff, made no attempt to hide his support for the ABM. Even when the president was on record as opposed to the system, Wheeler made public statements supporting it and criticizing the administration.

Supporting the services were several senior members of the Senate Armed Services Committee, including the chairman, Richard B. Russell, and such other influential members as John Stennis and Henry Jackson. These senators were supporters of Johnson's Vietnam policy and had been friends of the president when he was Democratic leader in the Senate during the Eisenhower Adminstration. Indeed, Johnson had served with them on Armed Services and trusted their judgment. He was particularly close to Russell.

In arguing their case, proponents and adversaries often stressed different factors. Supporters stressed the fact that the Soviets had already developed such a system, that it threatened America's deterrent capacity, and that the ABM would save American lives. The issue of arms limitations talks was not paramount to them. To the extent that they even considered this issue, they argued that an ABM would provide the Americans with an extra bargaining chip in any negotiations on mutual defensive weapons limitations. Opponents, on the other hand, were less concerned about the possibility of Soviet possession of ABMs than they were about the potential for a new arms race. Another factor that concerned the opponents more than the supporters was the price tag. Estimates of the cost of an ABM system ranged from $30 billion to $40 billion. By 1966, even with an unusually large congressional majority, Johnson was experiencing difficulties mobilizing Congress to approve funding for many of the social welfare programs of his Great Society package. With a sharply reduced majority in Congress in 1967, even greater difficulties were anticipated. Many opponents of the ABM—and, indeed, even Johnson—realized that any increase in the military budget could come only at the expense of decreased spending for social welfare programs. Since most of the supporters of the ABM were opposed to Johnson's Great Society package, this aspect of the problem did not trouble them.

Johnson was thus torn between the arguments made by his friends in the Senate that the ABM was needed for the national security and those of McNamara and Rusk that the system was likely to initiate a new arms race. Therefore, he was willing to postpone a decision. Two factors seem to have been particularly important in this respect. The first was that Johnson believed that an arms limitations agreement with the Soviets could change the opinion of the public—and of historians at a later date—on the foreign policy of his administration. Johnson's years in office had been dominated by a seemingly endless war in Vietnam, and the president was hoping for a major breakthrough in some area of international reconciliation. Second, the president wanted to avoid, if at all possible, a direct break with NcNamara. The two men were already at odds over Vietnam, but the president still valued his secretary of defense too highly to reject his advice out of hand. Since McNamara viewed the ABM choice as a direct confrontation between himself and the Joint Chiefs of Staff, a decision to deploy the system would be taken as a direct rebuff to the secretary. On the other hand, a negative decision on the ABM would alienate key senators who might proceed to wreak havoc with Johnson's domestic program. While these senators probably opposed much of the Great Society legislation anyway, a negative decision on the ABM might serve to antagonize them still further and thus provoke a sustained effort to cut back domestic programs. Not surprisingly, then, Johnson's instincts "led him to search for a compromise which would minimize the damage to his relations with his advisers."[21]

Ideally, the president would have preferred to let the supporters and opponents reach some kind of compromise among themselves. This was very much the Johnson style—that of the ultimate bargainer—which had been responsible for his tremendous popularity as Senate Democratic leader. It was also the style of Johnson's political mentor, Franklin D. Roosevelt. This course was simply not possible. As Hilsman has argued, a major consequence of "the multiplicity of constituencies involved in [foreign and defense] policy-making is that more and more problems are thrown into the White House. It is only the presidency . . . that can consider the whole broad range of interconnections between conflicting interests and demands."[22] The president's only recourse was to make another "minimal decision," one that would not identify either side as a "winner" or a "loser" but would represent some compromise among the competing positions.

The critical question thus became: What would be the nature of this compromise? At least a part of the answer became clear in a meeting Johnson and McNamara had with Soviet Premier Kosygin at Glassboro, New Jersey, in June, 1967. Johnson pressed the Soviets for a date for the opening of arms limitations talks but did not receive an answer. Kosygin, in a meeting with both Johnson and McNamara, described the Soviet ABM as a defensive weapon and therefore unobjectionable, hence not a proper subject for arms limitations talks. McNamara's principal objection to the ABM had now been refuted by the Soviets. Consequently, Johnson no longer saw the American ABM as a possible stumbling block to beginning arms limitations talks.[23]

The president was also worried about the possible electoral consequences of a negative decision on the ABM. In late 1966, Michigan Governor George Romney—then believed to be the front-runner for the Republican presidential nomination in 1968—discussed the ABM gap with the Soviet Union on national television. He also indicated that it would be a major issue in the 1968 campaign. Other Republicans made similar charges in Congress. Johnson wanted to quell these complaints. As the vice-presidential candidate on the 1960 ticket

that had charged the Eisenhower Administration with ne-
glecting the problem of an offensive missile gap, he knew that
the issue could be powerful. And it could lead to his own
defeat.

Even though the pressure for an ABM from the military and
Congress far outweighed the countervailing pressure from
McNamara and Rusk, the president was still committed to
seeking a compromise. Although the secretary of defense understood the pressures for a decision to deploy the ABM, he
remained steadfastly opposed to an anti-Soviet system, which
he believed might affect the possibility of an arms control
agreement. On September 18, 1967, McNamara announced
the administration's opposition to any major ABM deployment:

> The [Soviet ABM] system does not impose any threat to our
> ability to penetrate and inflict massive and unacceptable dam-
> age on the Soviet Union. In other words, it does not presently
> affect in any significant manner our assured destruction abil-
> ity. . . . While we have substantially improved our technology in
> the field, it is important to understand that none of the systems
> at the present or foreseeable state-of-the-art would provide an
> impenetrable shield over the United States . . . the $40 billion is
> not the issue. The money in itself is not the problem. . . . The
> point for us to keep in mind is that should the [arms limitations]
> talks fail—and the Soviets decide to expand their present mod-
> est ABM deployment into a massive one—our response must be
> realistic . . . if the Soviets elect to deploy a heavy ABM system,
> we must further expand our sophisticated offensive forces.[24]

In brief, not only could an ABM not protect the public, but it
could be overcome by saturating the defensive missiles' capability with a large number of ICBMs. If the United States could
overcome a Soviet ABM system in this way, presumably the
Russians could do the same should the United States deploy a
"thick" shield. On the other hand, McNamara came out for an
anti-Chinese ABM—in case the Chinese, who were at the time
perceived as militantly ideological and revolutionary, might
be just irrational enough to attempt a nuclear attack upon the
United States or its allies in Asia. The new system, called the
Sentinel, would have as its major function the defense of
American cities.

McNamara's speech clearly indicated that any American reaction to an increased Soviet buildup of the ABM system would
be countered by an American increase in offensive missiles.
This was a major victory for the secretary against the Joint
Chiefs of Staff and ABM supporters in Congress, who favored
the more extensive (and more expensive) ABM. The projected
cost of the Sentinel was approximately $5 billion. The very fact
that McNamara made the speech announcing the administration's support for the ABM indicated that he had by no means
suffered a major defeat on this issue. He could view the president's decision as leaving open the possibility that the system
would never be deployed at all if the Russians would agree to
a mutal defense weapons limitation. The administration had
not come out in support of deployment, but only for increased
funding for the procurement of certain ABM parts, which
would require a long lead-time. On the other hand, the very
fact that the administration had publicly changed its position
represented a victory for ABM supporters in Congress and the
Joint Chiefs. Proponents of a more extensive "thick" system
viewed the administration's change in position as a hopeful
sign and expected that they could accomplish their goal later.

Johnson had indeed made another minimal decision, a decision to postpone the real decision, and in so doing he came as
close to "partisan mutual adjustment" as was possible. This is
evident from McNamara's arguments on behalf of Sentinel.
The interjection of the Chinese threat into the argument
seemed to belie the administration's real reasons for supporting the ABM. The Chinese nuclear threat was hardly overwhelming in the fall of 1967: The first atomic bomb was
detonated by China in 1964, the next one a year later. In 1965,
the Chinese were reported to have detonated two hydrogen
bombs, and a third in the spring of 1967. For someone as
committed to programs with demonstrated cost-effectiveness,
it certainly appeared strange to find McNamara proposing a
multi-billion dollar system to oppose what was essentially a
minor threat. Clearly, the real purpose of stressing the anti-
Chinese nature of the American ABM was to restrict the overall scope of any possible future deployment and especially to
prevent the creation of a "thick," anti-Soviet shield.
McNamara was particularly anxious to impress the distinction
between an anti-Soviet and an anti-Chinese system on Ameri-

can public opinion and mobilize support for the "thin" system. He was also very concerned to communicate this difference to the Kremlin, lest it continue to oppose strategic arms limitation talks and initiate a new offensive arms spiral. Another argument in McNamara's speech is worth noting: the secretary's statement that "the $40 billion is not the issue." Why was it not the issue? Not because Johnson would have been willing to spend that much for an ABM if necessary, but rather because the Sentinel decision no longer required massive outlays of funds. The new program did not dramatically increase the level of defense spending; the estimated cost of $5 billion would not become a major issue until a decision to deploy the Sentinel was made.

The critical point is that McNamara's speech did not address the main arguments of either proponents or opponents of the ABM: The threat of the Soviet ABMs was simply denied in two sentences; the impact of the new system on the potential for arms limitations talks was not even mentioned; the question of national priorities was barely alluded to (by the reference to the $40-billion cost of Nike-X), and the feasibility of the Sentinel system was totally ignored. Under a rational actor model, we would have expected these questions to form the basis for a speech either accepting or rejecting the ABM. They did not. Instead, a side issue—the Chinese "threat"—was made the central concern. Neither the proponents nor the opponents had used this argument in earlier debates over the ABM. The introduction of this argument for Sentinel clearly represented an attempt to find an ex post facto rationale to fit a decision that had been arrived at on the basis of domestic political considerations rather than strategic ones. The Chinese nuclear threat was clearly a "minimal" problem which could be solved by a "minimal" decision. The compromise Johnson was able to reach was hardly satisfactory to any side—but compromises never are. By letting participants outside the executive branch play a major role in determining defense policy, the president had skillfully maneuvered a compromise that neither the supporters nor the opponents of the ABM could reject without risking further losses.

The ABM decision under Johnson thus is a good example of the bureaucratic model. There was, indeed, a multiplicity of

actors in the decision-making arena. In contrast to crisis decision-making, not only did Congress play a role on the ABM, but
the legislative branch was able to reverse the position the
president himself had held. Secondly, the program decision
took a considerable amount of time to be reached. An ABM
system had first been proposed in the mid-1950s; Johnson did
not act until 1967. Many program policies are resolved in
shorter periods: Since the defense budget is annual, at least
some programs are reevaluated in a relatively short time span.
On the other hand, domestic programs may take even longer:
Comprehensive federal aid to education and a system of gov-
ernment-subsidized health care for the aged had each been
under consideration in Congress for more than fifty years before Johnson maneuvered them through the 89th Congress in
1965. And finally, the various actors may view the stakes in
different ways, a situation which makes compromises possible
and minimal decisions likely. The 1967 decision by Johnson let
McNamara still believe that the arms race could be limited and
let the Joint Chiefs still hope for an expanded ABM. As in all
bargaining situations that are successfull terminated, neither
side saw itself as a clear loser. In the process of reaching a
compromise, however, the value-maximizing approach of the
rational actor model was left behind. The 1967 decision did not
appear to maximize any of the original values posed by either
supporters or opponents of the ABM. Indeed, factors that have
no place in a strategic decision made on the basis of rational
calculations—such as domestic political considerations—appear to have been dominant in the bureaucratic politics of the
Johnson decision.

THE RATIONAL ACTOR MODEL AND PROGRAM POLICIES: NIXON AND THE ABM

Johnson's decision to support ABM development and procurement of parts clearly did not resolve the long-range problem of whether or not to deploy the Sentinel (or some
alternative system). When Johnson decided not to run for reelection, the problem was passed to the next administration. It
was certainly conceivable that Nixon might attempt to reach

some sort of compromise on the ABM, but he chose not to do so. Johnson's ABM decision was made in the light of the diverse goals of the various actors involved. Nixon, on the other hand, stipulated a goal—providing an adequate defense against the increasing Soviet offensive capability—and then proceeded to seek the most effective way of maximizing it. In so doing, he chose to raise the stakes of the decision by interjecting the Soviet threat into the debate again. In contrast to Johnson, who delighted in using his skills at bargaining, Nixon justified virtually all of his policy decisions (on both foreign and domestic issues) on the basis of some stipulated goal. He then would lay out the possible means of achieving it and select the one he thought most likely to do so. Nixon would then confront Congress with a choice of either accepting his solution or acting irresponsibly and irrationally. At times—such as on the issues of impounding funds appropriated by Congress and legislative attempts to cut off funds for the war in Southeast Asia—the president simply told Congress that he would not follow any policy other than the one he had proposed.

Nixon's decision to deploy an ABM was his first direct confrontation with Congress. The president announced his decision on March 14, 1969, less than two months after his inauguration. In testimony before the Senate Armed Services Committee five days later, Secretary of Defense Melvin Laird stated that the administration had considered four alternatives.[25] The first was a deployment that would defend major American cities against a Soviet attack; it was rejected because it was not feasible. No defense could prevent a catastrophic level of American casualties. In addition, as Nixon stressed, to protect American cities might appear to the Soviets as a prelude to an American attack and therefore provoke a preemptive Soviet first strike. The second alternative called for no deployment at all, but a continuation of research and development on the ABM; the third provided for the continuation of Johnson's Sentinel program. Both of these were rejected because they would not provide sufficient protection against the rapidly increasing buildup of Soviet land-based missiles. By 1969, the number of these Soviet missiles had exceeded the counterpart American force. The final alternative was the development of a modified system that would defend a nucleus of land-based strategic missiles against a Soviet first strike, in essence "safeguarding" the retaliatory capacity of the United States. This system would also provide a defense against a possible small Chinese attack. Having eliminated all but one possibility, the administration's only option was the fourth alternative.

The new Safeguard system did represent some compromises between the more extensive system urged by the Joint Chiefs of Staff and the position of the ABM opponents. Having made these compromises, however, Nixon was not prepared to go any farther. Congress would be faced with either accepting or rejecting Safeguard as proposed. The decision to reject defense of major cities, which the Joint Chiefs had favored, is instructive in this respect. The heavier system was rejected because it was not technologically feasible and might provoke a Soviet preemptive strike. Many congressmen had also complained to Johnson that their constituents did not want ABM installations in their districts. Yet there were congressmen who had taken just the opposite position: They wanted their constituents to be safe from any nuclear attack and would welcome an ABM site in their districts.[26] Nixon probably remembered the fight that Johnson had had over the Model Cities program. Johnson had problems lining up congressional support for the program, originally designed to make a few cities demonstrations of how ingenuity, dedication, and technology could change an urban area, unless each member whose vote he sought was promised that his district would have a "model city." During the coalition-building process, the number of "model cities" soared and the entire nature of the program had to be altered. What started out as an experiment in social engineering ended as a prime example of pork-barrel politics. Nixon was thus putting Congress on notice that the ABM was not subject to logrolling. The administration would not provide a congressman with a guarantee of an ABM in his district if he would vote for the project.

The interjection of the Soviet threat into the arguments supporting ABM deployment served to crystallize the debate in Congress about the new weapons system—and, in addition, to demonstrate that rational decision-making does not necessarily mean that all who examine various alternatives agree

that the means selected are the best and most desirable way
of achieving the designated end. Whereas the administration
argued that the ABM would enhance national security by en-
suring that the nation's retaliatory capacity could not be de-
stroyed, opponents charged that Safeguard was unnecessary
because the United States possessed not only Minutemen but
also a large force of bombers and Polaris submarines. Thus,
while a Soviet first strike might be able to inflict real damage
on these forces, it could not possibly wipe out the American
capacity to launch a second strike that would totally destroy
the Soviet Union. Whereas the proponents of the ABM argued
that its deployment would not endanger arms limitations talks
since the Soviets, after all, already possessed ABMs and considered them defensive weapons, their adversaries asserted that
deployment would indeed obstruct any talks. While Nixon and
Laird argued that protection of American land-based missiles
was defensive and did not endanger Moscow's ability to deter
the United States by threatening the obliteration of American
cities, the congressional critics argued that an ABM would
indeed initiate a new arms race by precipitating a further
Soviet ICBM buildup. Both supporters and opponents of the
ABM, then, accepted the foreign policy goal of providing an
adequate defense against the Soviet (and Chinese) ICBMs as
the one to be maximized. The debate centered upon one question: Did the Nixon Administration choose the best alternative
to do so?

Nixon's decision to make the ABM a priority item on his
legislative agenda further raised the stakes of the decision and
made it more apparent than ever that the final choice would
involve both "winners" and "losers." There would be no compromise on the ABM, and indeed none was proposed in Congress. (An attempt was made to limit the funding to research
and development, but had this motion passed it would have
effectively killed the Safeguard.) This refusal to compromise,
together with Nixon's general "get-tough" attitude toward
Congress, served to solidify the coalitions supporting and opposing the ABM. These coalitions were apparent even in early
1967, when the issue of an anti-Soviet ABM was still unresolved.[27] A sizable bloc in Congress opposed any such anti-
Soviet system but was willing to support the Johnson

compromise of a limited anti-Chinese ABM. The opponents of an anti-Soviet system in 1967 appeared to have maintained this position two years later. The two sides were becoming increasingly clear. By the time of the key roll call vote in the Senate—in August, 1969—only a handful of senators remained either undecided or publicly uncommitted. It was clear even in March that the Senate vote would be very close—a fact which seemed to raise the stakes of the issue even higher.

Supporting Safeguard were the administration, the military, the defense contractors, scientists at Rand and at the Hudson Institute, and the bloc on the Senate Armed Services Committee that had pushed so hard for an ABM under Johnson (Stennis was now chairman, following the death of Russell). Most of the opposition to the ABM was found in Congress itself. Senate Majority Leader Mansfield, Majority Whip Edward M. Kennedy (D., Mass.), and Foreign Relations Committee Chairman Fulbright led the opposition forces. Media criticism of the system was also widespread, as major newspapers such as the *New York Times,* the *Washington Post,* the *St. Louis Post-Dispatch,* and the *Boston Globe* took positions of vigorous opposition. Kennedy organized his own group of scientists and scholars in opposition to deployment: The group issued a book of short essays outlining the various arguments against the ABM. Indeed, even public opinion began to play a role. Several members of Congress stated publicly that they would follow the dictates of their constituents (as reflected by the mail they received) on the final votes in 1969. Gallup polls taken on April 6 and July 27, 1969, indicated that 69 percent of the respondents had either heard about or read about the ABM, a rather high figure.[28] The two surveys did not, however, indicate that the ABM divided public opinion into two warring factions: Only 40 percent of each sample had formed an opinion on the program, with a majority in support of Safeguard in both samples.

Nixon himself generated much controversy by his approach to senators who had not firmy made up their minds. He reportedly threatened at least one Republican leaning against the ABM with supporting a primary opponent in the senator's next election. While a rational actor model would not predict that attempts to win votes for a cause would be made through vote-trading, the model does not assume that the conflict between potential winners and losers is necessarily that acute. Nixon's own style undoubtedly contributed to raising the stakes of the ABM issue, as well as those of many other issues in his tenure in office. The president strongly believed in the Safeguard proposal; indeed, he thought it to be the only rational course of action possible. As such, he was willing to press quite hard for it, even at the expense of alienating potential supporters. Johnson, on the other hand, disliked the use of pressure tactics. When a bargain could be made, he made it.

The president's position prevailed, but only by a two-vote margin in the August 6, 1969, Senate vote. The House took three votes on the ABM, the closest of which came on a procedural amendment and had 223 supporters of Safeguard and 141 opponents. Despite Nixon's insistence that Safeguard would not be expanded into a "thick" ABM, an analysis of the 1969 House votes showed that most of the support for Nixon's ABM came from members who two years ealier had voiced support for a $30-billion Nike-X.[29] The basic pattern of cleavage, then, seems not to have changed very much from the period immediately preceding Johnson's endorsement of an anti-Chinese ABM. The arguments used by each side had, if anything, been made more explicit by Nixon. Especially when considered in this light, Johnson's decision was "minimal" at best.

The ABM saga came to an end in late 1975, when the Senate voted 52-47 to dismantle the site at Langdon, North Dakota. The Ford Administration opposed the move, but the Congressional response was based upon the SALT agreement with the Soviet Union limiting the number of ABM installations each country could build to two, one protecting missiles and the other protecting the nation's capital. Furthermore, in 1974, the United States and the Soviets agreed to cut back the number of ABM installations to one for each country. The United States had originally proposed a limit of four sites at the SALT talks, but it was the Soviet Union that had insisted upon the maximum of two. The latter figure would allow each country to build only one additional site—to meet what the other nation already had. The limitation to one site apiece reached in 1974 reflected the fact that neither country was anxious to engage in further construction of the expensive bases. In retrospect, Johnson's support for a modest ABM system as a negotiating tool with the Soviets on a more general arms limitation agreement (which had not yet been reached) proved to be correct—yet, the decision to build a moderate system was not at all based upon the original Johnson logic! It is fitting that the Democratic Congress which had insisted upon ABM development for such a long period would finally go against a president who supported Safeguard and vote to dismantle the system.

Most of the Senators who participated in the 1969 vote (on which all 100 members voted) were still in the Senate on November 18, 1975, when 99 members cast ballots on the motion to dismantle the system. Only eight members changed their votes, five in favor of keeping the system and three moving towards opposition. Of the five who became pro-ABM, only one was a Republican; the others were all Western Democrats, whose states benefited from contracts and subcontracts for the system. A particularly notable change was that of Senator Quentin Burdick (D., N.D.), a 1969 opponent of the ABM. Dismantling the lone system, however, would mean that Langdon's population would drop from its boom level of 4800 to 2800; it was 2300 before ABM installation began. While North Dakota's other senator, Milton Young, was a strong supporter of the ABM from the beginning, Burdick's position changed to protect the interests of his constituents. By 1975, most of the original opponents of the ABM were more convinced than ever that the program was nothing but a large pork barrel program for the military. Supporters maintained that the military value of the system was still critical. What accounted for the change in the outcome of the Senate vote? The answer is straightforward: Democrats had picked up several new seats since the 1969 vote and what turnover there was went overwhelmingly against the ABM. The ABM had served the purpose intended for it by Johnson and could be scrapped. The only irony involved is that the Democrats who provided the margin to dismantle the system had run for office opposing the policies in international politics that Johnson had espoused.

The ABM thus became defused as a major issue in pretty much the same way it had been initiated—through bureau-

cratic politics in which different actors saw alternative justifica-
tions for similar positions. We now turn to a situation in which
there are even more actors involved and in which the perceptions of what stakes are involved vary considerably from one
actor to another. If anything, this makes decision-making even
more complex to understand and more difficult to achieve.

"INTERMESTIC" POLICIES: DIFFERENT STAKES FOR DIFFERENT FOLKS

We have discussed "intermestic" policies at some length,
but have not specified the sets of relationships that are found
among the actors on those policies which had long been considered entirely within the domestic sphere. In this chapter,
we have presented two models of the policy-making process,
the "rational actor" approach and "bureaucratic politics."
Most program policies are best described by the bureaucratic
model, whereas crisis decisions are better explained by the
rational actor model. Yet, this distinction is not valid for all
foreign policy decisions, as our discussion of the ABM makes
clear. The critical element in determining which model is most
appropriate is the number of actors involved. When we move
beyond the first circle, the potential for decision-making on
the basis of rational criteria becomes less likely. The larger the
number of actors involved, the less likely it is that each will
perceive the stakes in the same way.

On intermestic policies, there are a large number of actors
involved. And, as one might expect, there is often little common ground on which policy decisions might be made. In fact,
there is so little common ground that intermestic policies often
cannot be identified with any overall policy. Energy is a prime
case in point. For almost a century, we have been warned that
our resources are in danger of imminent depletion. Yet, new
supplies of oil and coal, both available inexpensively and abun-
dantly, were always discovered, and technological advances
made these resources available at levels which outpaced the
new demands. There was little conflict between nations, since
the industrialized countries held the rights for oil development in the lesser-developed countries; there were few do-

mestic problems since the oil, coal, and natural gas industries each had their own markets. Occasionally, tax reformers would challenge the oil depletion allowance, but did not meet with any success. The energy situation before 1973 fit very well into the low intensity situation as described by E. E. Schattschneider, which explains the lack of conflict on that policy area.[30] There was no comprehensive energy policy because no one saw the need for one.

Since 1973, as the question of energy became increasingly salient, the number of actors dramatically increased. Now, the lack of a comprehensive energy policy can be explained by too many conflicting goals, too diverse to reconcile so that a single set of problems which could clearly be put into a context that permitted a "rational decision" would emerge. To see the nature of the problem, let us consider the actors involved on energy policy. First, there are the nations in which the bulk of the world's oil is to be found; they have banded together in a cartel to fix prices at a level considerably in excess of pre-1973 costs. The Organization of Petroleum Exporting Countries (OPEC) is largely, though not exclusively, made up of Arab nations in the Middle East. These nations imposed an oil embargo in 1973 on those countries, including the United States, which supported Israel in the recent war. Yet, the Arab nations differed in the extent of their opposition to Israel, their own preferences for foreign allies, and the extent to which each needed a constant cash flow from oil to maintain a desired level of economic growth. Second, the oil companies, as well as the coal and natural gas producers, are major actors on energy matters. But, producers of alternative sources of energy, particularly in a period of shortage, are each concerned with their own markets. They are competitors and, as we found in trade legislation and on the debate on the ABM under Johnson, each is likely to perceive only those aspects of the energy problem which are relevant to their own situations. To the extent that oil is in competition with natural gas, for example, the producers will be more likely to oppose each other than to constitute a united front called "business." Note further that the oil companies, in particular, are largely multinational corporations. Their interests and their bases of operation are only partially within the borders of the United States. Thus, they are less subject to regulation in their activities (such as the bribing of foreign officials or participation in the Arab boycott of Israel), which can be channeled through foreign subsidiaries. As a last resort, they could threaten to move their corporate headquarters out of the United States and thus be only minimally subject to American regulations.

A third group of actors are minor producers of energy, ranging from small oil companies to the new solar energy firms. Small oil companies have not traditionally benefited from the tax advantages under the depletion allowance. The depletion allowance permits an oil company to obtain tax advantages on exploratory drillings. In 1975 the Congress finally restricted the depletion allowance, despite years of strong lobbying against such a move by the major oil producers. A fourth group is the environmentalists, who have stressed the need to clean up the nation's air, water, and land resources. They have pressed for strip-mining controls (opposed by coal producers), passed twice by Congress but vetoed by Ford both times in 1976; with Carter's support, a modified bill became law in 1977. They have also worked for environmental safeguards to prevent oil slicks and to reduce the level of pollution produced by the internal combustion engine which powers the automobile. A fifth group is public opinion and a sixth is the Congress. With respect to the environment, Congress sensed a strong popular demand in the 1960s and early 1970s for environmental protection legislation and adopted strict new pollution codes without considering whether it was possible to meet the new standards or what the implications for energy resources might be.[31] Since 1973, it has also felt popular pressure to hold energy prices down and even look for scapegoats. A seventh set of actors, the automobile producers (multinational corporations themselves), saw the stakes quite differently from most of the other actors. They were concerned with the relative sales figures of large versus small cars during the energy crisis of 1973—and the decision they reached in 1973 was changed in the next few years, as supplies of oil increased following the boycott and motorists no longer had to stand on line at gas stations. An eighth actor was the Environmental Protection Agency, which had to rule on the compliance of automobile manufacturers with environmental guidelines, as well as investigating the safety of nuclear power. The question of nuclear power, of course, also brought both domestic and military actors (the Atomic Energy Commission and the various services), into the realm of energy policy as a ninth set of actors. A tenth thus became the entire community (producers, sellers, arms control agencies) involved in nuclear power and the possibility that proliferation might lead to a greater potential for war. Finally, there is the president, who must consider all of these potential actors in the many aspects of energy policy.

Each of these actors sees only part of the larger picture of energy policy, with the possible exception of the president who may try to coordinate these alternative perspectives into something resembling a comprehensive policy. However, the difficulties in accomplishing this can be seen by noting that not only are many actors involved—seeing things from different perspectives—but there is no clear-cut position as to what the stakes are on something we call "energy policy." Environmentalists worry about the pollution of our natural resources and possible limits to the growth of technology. Oil companies (despite their advertisements) are not overly concerned with the effects of an energy policy on the environment, but are more deeply concerned with the questions of: (1) their own economic interests on the domestic front (as in the case of the tax structure); and (2) American relations with OPEC nations. The Environmental Protection Agency is primarily concerned with the domestic ramifications of nuclear energy and does not get involved in questions of nuclear proliferation among other countries in the world. Thus, some groups see the formulation of energy policy in primarily domestic terms, others as a major foreign policy consideration, and some as increasingly intermestic. Yet, there is hardly a consensus on what the energy policy should be. Nor is there evidence that many groups would be willing to sacrifice their own interests in the name of a coordinated energy policy. Energy producers become concerned with foreign policy stakes only when they deal with foreign markets; the American coal industry has, instead, concentrated upon expanding its own domestic market. Many oil companies have become increasingly involved in foreign policy questions, urging greater American support for the Arabs in the Middle East but also pressing for a reconciliation with

Vietnam and Angola, both of which have large oil reserves. The stakes involved in energy policy range across the entire gamut, but each actor only sees with clarity those directly relating to its immediate interests.

We have not presented a case study of conflict over energy policy because it is simply too difficult to state what a single energy policy might be. The number of actors involved is extremely large, encompassing all four circles. Interests sometimes conflict with each other; more often than not they crisscross, as each actor sees only part of the larger issue. For example, Reps. Bob Krueger and Bob Eckhardt (both Texas Democrats) led the battle (for and against, respectively) on decontrol of natural gas prices in 1976. In 1977, they worked together to pass an amendment to Carter's emergency decontrol bill. The amendment ensured that the interstate price would not exceed the price charged within Texas! Energy politics made strange political alliances. Most of the other actors stood by indifferently, since their own interests were not involved. The politics of energy is marked by bureaucratic politics to a greater extent than any "purely" domestic program, since it involves so many actors, both domestic and international. There are so many governmental bureaucracies involved (Atomic Energy Commission, Environmental Protection Agency, the various boards monitoring oil, natural gas, and coal production, Arms Control and Disarmanent Agency, etc.) that it is simply a mistake to speak of a government policy.

Food policy, which involves the president, bureaucracies, Congress, and public opinion, is similarly complex. The Agriculture committees in the House and Senate are concerned not only with price supports and export and import quotas, but also new questions of how much of particular commodities should be stockpiled, control over the weather (to the extent possible)—which determines the ability of the United States to export and stockpile commodities, the food stamp program, and nutrition for the nation's children. They must also be concerned with new technologies for increasing crop yields and new sources of food. These concerns do not even begin to tap the wider international ramifications of food policy. Does the United States, as the world's largest food exporter, have a moral obligation to feed the people of the developing nations?

Or, do we keep our food reserves stockpiled in the event of a long-term drought, as almost occurred in 1977? Do we use our food resources—and, if so, to what extent—to insure detente with the Soviet Union or as a weapon against the threat of another oil embargo? Intermestic policies involve so many actors and so many complex questions that it simply does not make sense to speak of "comprehensive" policies—or models to explain them. Policies have become disjointed because there are so many interests involved. Bureaucratic politics over limited objectives leads to the adoption of policies reached by compromise. On the new intermestic policies, one hardly knows where to begin to propose either a rational solution (if one exists) or a compromise which will be acceptable to a sufficient number of actors.

In presenting the two models of decision-making, we have stressed that the models are conceptual devices for interpreting foreign policy decisions. Crisis decision-making seems to follow the rational actor model quite well. However, as we have argued, program policies may follow either the bureaucratic or the rational actor model. Which model best explains a given decision can be determined only by examining the interactions of the decision-makers and how each coalition views the stakes involved. Many program decisions, such as specific allocations in the defense budget, never reach the president directly: These are the most likely to involve bargaining and compromises. Which model most appropriately analyzes a program decision that does reach the president, such as the two ABM decisions, is determined to a large extent by the president's own style and his relations with other actors.

It is at this stage, however, that we reach a paradox. The opinion conversion notion of representation discussed in the previous chapter becomes most critical in issues that have the most pronounced consequences: crisis decisions. However, it is precisely on these types of issues that public opinion has tended to follow rather than lead the president. The president is virtually a free agent in crisis decisions, while his actions are more limited on such less critical issues (in terms of the stakes involved) as defense spending and ABM deployment. Conversely, Congress is weakest where the president is strongest: in crisis decisions. When it attempts to check the president, as it did in 1973 on the bombing of Cambodia, it faces the presidential charge that it is trespassing on the duties of the commander-in-chief. If the impact of public opinion and congressional oversight is most critical but also weakest on crisis decisions, what can we say about the democratic character of foreign policy decision-making? The problem becomes particularly acute in the context of limited wars and in situations in which the president can "declare" a crisis without consulting Congress (as Johnson did, for example, in the Dominican Republic in 1965). And, perhaps most problematic of all will be the questions involving "intermestic" issues. These issues seem to demand carefully planned rational policies; yet the number of different actors involved, many of whom see the stakes primarily in terms of domestic politics, makes a bureaucratic solution appear almost inevitable. Can the president proclaim an "energy crisis," even in the event of a national emergency such as another oil embargo? If so, what measures can he take without waiting for the slow process of congressional approval to legitimize them? It is to this fundamental tension in the conduct of foreign policy in a democracy—a conflict which is likely to increase substantially in coming years—that we now turn.

5

BALANCING THE SCALES?

WHAT KIND OF CONGRESS?

The Great Depression, followed by the New Deal and the Nazi threat, followed after Germany's defeat by the cold war, all contributed to the steady accretion of presidential power. But for the Vietnam War, this unchallenged growth might have continued. This trend toward increasing presidential power had gone unchallenged because crisis after crisis, domestic and foreign, required strong action and often speedy reaction. The need for a powerful presidency seemed obvious. More than that, the growth of presidential power was identified with the use of this power domestically for progressive social legislation (New Deal, Fair Deal, New Frontier, and Great Society programs) and externally for the defense of what used to be called the Free World, although it included non-democratic societies. The confrontation of Stalin's Russia—which, not surprisingly so soon after World War II, looked a lot like Hitler's Germany to Western eyes—with the United States, Britain, and France made the cold war appear to be fundamentally a continuing struggle of totalitarianism against democracy. Thus the expansion of presidential power was identified with liberal causes, with domestic changes to help the underprivileged and to correct social injustices, and a foreign policy to protect liberal values that had just been assaulted by Hitler and were now being assaulted by Stalin. In

fact, it had simply come to be assumed that the president is a
liberal and that, therefore, he can, like the kings of old, "do no
wrong."

During those days it was conservatives who opposed the
trend toward increasing presidential power; as exponents of
little government and congressional supremacy, they opposed
New Deal and other domestic reforms, as well as the conduct
of a vigorous foreign policy, all of which required Big Government, especially Big Executive Government. Liberals cham-
pioned the latter. But Vietnam reversed the liberal attitudes
toward presidential power. Liberals, who had always expected
"their" presidents to back good causes whether eliminating
poverty, doing away with racial injustice, or stopping totalitarian aggression, became schizophrenic as the war escalated.
Johnson's domestic record surpassed that of John F. Kennedy,
whose style and charm attracted liberals but who by the time
of his death had not managed to get Congress to pass even one
piece of major social legislation; Johnson got it passed and then
began passing his own set of reforms. But Vietnam disillu-
sioned many liberals. A war in defense of an undemocratic
government, often fought by methods that repelled men of
humane sentiments, springing from commitments made by
Presidents Eisenhower and Kennedy and transformed into a
major war by Johnson, not only seemed incompatible with the
very values America proclaimed to the world but was carried
on in a way that seemed unconstitutional.

The Gulf of Tonkin resolution, the blank check Congress
gave Johnson but did not expect him to use to initiate a large
land war in Asia, only made the war an even more bitter
experience. Vietnam, a "presidential war," was perceived to
be the culmination of the trend toward increasingly powerful
presidents who were not subject to the legislative restraint
envisaged by the Founding Fathers; had they not with good
reason, in the Constitution, specifically provided against the
danger of locating absolute power in the hands of one man by
assigning to Congress the authority to "declare war" and the
president the authority to "make war"? In the future, asked
New York Times journalist Tom Wicker, a critic, "could a president, for example, bomb Lima in order to forestall or retaliate
for some act of expropriation by Peru? If Fidel Castro refuses

to help put an end to airline hijackings to Cuba, can Mr. Nixon constitutionally bomb Havana to make him negotiate seriously?"[1] Does not the present Constitution, amended by years of presidential practice and congressional acquiescence, read in effect: "The president may conduct a war unless Congress halts him"? Hence, to redress the balance between the executive and legislative, to prevent another Vietnam and avoid a second costly disaster and strain of the American social fabric, a flood of proposals has been put forward, almost all of which aim at a greater role in the making of foreign policy, and especially the use of force, for Congress—and, through it, presumably "the people."

The belief that the presidency—when occupied by bellicose presidents—needs to be restrained by a pacific Congress, acting as the representative of the people, assumes that Congress, especially the Senate, would demonstrate wisdom, moderation, and virtue, qualities that have frequently been lacking in the postwar period.

> This spring the land is filled. . . .with a resounding chorus demanding that the United States Senate reassert its "right" over foreign policy. . . .
>
> But, hold on a moment. Which Senate are we speaking of? Are we talking of the Senate which has over and over again balked at constructive foreign initiative, crippled foreign efforts, ignored foreign opportunities? Are we talking of the Senate which blocked American entry into the League of Nations, held back full support for the World Court, is presently cutting back further and further on foreign aid, which has no hesitation over passing resolutions mixing in the affairs of other countries for political rather than diplomatic reasons?
>
> Of course, this is not the Senate which today's "strengthen-the-Senate" advocates have in mind. They visualize an upper chamber full of wisdom and goodwill, a bulwark of reason and foresight in a reckless world. In short, they dream of a Senate which will hew to their own concept of where foreign policy should go and how it should be conducted.[2]

However, these expectations are of a Congress whose foreign policy stance for most of the postwar period has been intensely anti-Communist and nationalistic. Presidents have therefore moved with great caution, if and when they have moved at all, in their relations with Communist countries lest they be tainted as "soft on communism." Even in the 1976 presidential campaign, for example, President Ford dropped the word "detente" as the key phrase describing Soviet-American relations. Ford and Carter both took a tough line on the issue of the Panama Canal, maintaining that the United States must keep complete control over the Canal Zone. Many critics of a new canal treaty worry that Panama would follow the lead of other Latin American countries and take a sharp turn to the left, thereby eliminating American control of this vital waterway. Carter did change his policy after his inauguration. Congress has generally been supportive of administrative initiatives in foreign policy, but in recent years there has been a movement toward an increased role for the legislative branch in the formulation of both foreign and domestic policy. Congress has adopted a set of internal reforms to facilitate a more independent role in policy-making, but it is not at all clear whether: (1) these reforms actually have actually helped or hinder the policy-making role;[3] and (2) the Congress will be more responsive to new foreign policy initiatives, instead of further restricting presidential moves to set new directions in our foreign policy.

Also, the view of Congress as a protective check on warlike presidents overlooks the fact that Congress approved U.S. participation in both limited wars. Had President Truman requested a declaration of war after North Korea's invasion of South Korea, he would have received it; support for Truman's decision to intervene militarily with U.S. forces received virtually unanimous congressional and popular support. Only after the war became domestically unpopular did a few conservative senators raise the question of its constitutionality. Similarly, President Johnson had the support of large majorities in Congress and the country not only at the time of the Gulf of Tonkin incident during the summer of 1964 but also when the sustained bombing of North Vietnam began in the spring of 1965. If a War Powers Act had existed at the time, it would not have prevented either of the two limited wars in which the United States has become engaged since 1945. Nor would the rule that, sixty days after intervening, the president must desist if he does not receive legislative support after explaining his reason for intervening have changed these outcomes. For this would have been too short a period for any congressional investigation to turn up facts beyond those—as in the North Korean invasion—already evident or explained by the president; Congress's Tonkin Gulf investigation did turn up additional information—three years after the events.

If there is one rule that has become clear in the post-World War II period, it is that during real or alleged crises, Congress and the public turn to the president for information and interpretation. For example, it was Kennedy's interpretation of the impact of Russian missiles in Cuba that precipitated the Cuban missile crisis. Put in different words, the president has a superior ability to manipulate the picture of reality in the short run; this advantageous presidential position is reinforced by an emotional fact of life—namely, that if the president sends troops into action, be it in the name of freedom or security or both, the patriotic feelings that are aroused will make it extremely difficult to oppose him and refuse him the troops and money he requests. In fact, it will take a great deal more willingness on the part of Congress to accept responsibility for its decisions in case history should turn out to vindicate the president.

PRE-VIETNAM: ROOSEVELT AND HITLER

It was the war in Vietnam that led to the demands for congressional restraint of the president. Had the war not turned into a tragedy it is doubtful that any War Powers Act would ever have come before Congress. The act's purpose is to prevent another Vietnam, just as the Neutrality Laws of the 1930s were supposed to prevent American involvement in a second world war.

However strong the case for presidential restraint may seem in the wreckage and wake of Vietnam, and however persuasively it appears to reaffirm the rules under which the United States has in the past gone to war or argues for a new set of rules, perhaps a longer glance at history is in order before we conclude that the War Powers Act is a wise precaution. The period of 1940–41, the period from the fall of France to Pearl Harbor, may suggest quite a different answer.[4] For that was a period in which Congress still strongly represented isolationist sentiments, while the president became increasingly convinced that continued isolationism in the face of a Nazi Germany controlling most of continental Europe and threatening Britain with invasion and defeat would be a disastrous course. In view of the post-Vietnam American mood of at least some retraction from the global commitments of the cold war, if not an extensive withdrawal from the world to be matched by a concentration of attention and resources on domestic problems, the period 1940–41 may be of a significance at least equal to Vietnam's, and not just of historical interest.

England and the British navy had throughout most of the nineteenth century protected the United States and enabled it to focus on its own affairs—the continental expansion, the urbanization and industrialization of the country, and the socialization of the millions of immigrants who came to America looking for a better life. So in 1940 England's safety and keeping its navy out of German hands was of vital importance to American security. Just after the collapse of France in May, 1940, and Churchill's appointment as prime minister to succeed the discredited Chamberlain, the prime minister appealed to Roosevelt to send him destroyers to replace those already lost at sea convoying supplies bought in the United States and being taken to England on British and Canadian merchantmen. At a time of an expected German invasion, the British needed more destroyers to guard the convoys, for the rest of their destroyer force was concentrated around England to help repulse a German invasion across the English Channel if and when it came. But Congress was opposed to such a transfer. Despite the utter seriousness of the situation, the very great possibility of a British defeat should the Germans launch an invasion at any moment, despite repeated entreaties from Churchill and the urgings of his newly appointed Republican secretaries of war and navy, Roosevelt hesitated and procrastinated in the face of congressional opposition. Finally, after a delay of four crucial months, the president finally approved, and then only after an outside group called the Committee to Defend America by Aiding the Allies suggested the means: an executive agreement that bypassed Congress and disguised the sending of fifty old World War I-vintage destroyers to Britain as an act of strengthening America's hemispheric defense; in return the British leased to the United States bases in the Caribbean.

When Britain's cash reserves to pay for war supplies ran out, Roosevelt went to Congress for a lend-lease program, arguing that if the country continued to supply arms and munitions to Britain, it would improve Britain's ability to defend itself and help win the war; by becoming the "great arsenal of democracy," America would in all probability be able to avoid involvement in the war. Congress approved and thus helped solve Britain's financial problem at a time of peril. But when it came time to deliver the weapons, Congress balked. For by now, the spring of 1941, the Germans had launched an intensive submarine campaign against British ships on the Atlantic. With 500,000 tons of shipping a month being sunk in what came to be called throughout 1941 and 1942 the Battle of the Atlantic, it became clear that, if Britain was to survive, the supplies had to get across the ocean. Congress specifically forbade the president to authorize the use of U.S. warships as escorts.

His cabinet again urged him to do precisely that, but, as before, Roosevelt procrastinated even while he told the country that the delivery of arms to Britain was imperative. He would only extend the area the American navy patrolled in the Atlantic, informing Churchill that it would seek out German ships and report their presence to British convoys. But he would not commit himself to their escort. He briefly toyed with the idea that British ships could join U.S. convoys of supplies to the American troops that had been stationed in July, 1941, in Iceland (at the president's order) to prevent the capture of the island—the key to the supply route across the ocean —by the Nazis. This would have meant that U.S. warships could have escorted British ships better than halfway across the Atlantic, thereby greatly relieving the pressure on British destroyer escort capability. At one time Roosevelt gave the orders to the navy, only to withdraw them. Not until September, months after the enactment of lend-lease, did Roosevelt finally give the order and also announce that in the future U.S.

warships would "shoot-on-sight" at German warships and submarines; and then he did so only after he had told the public
that a German submarine had deliberately attacked the destroyer *Greer*, thus signaling a new policy of force by the Germans. In fact, the *Greer* had for several hours pursued a
German submarine, telling the British its position; the submarine finally turned on its relentless pursuer to get away. Roosevelt, in short, used the *Greer* incident as Johnson was to use the
Gulf of Tonkin events in August, 1964, to mobilize support for
his policies. Clearly it was necessary for American warships to
help convoy the supplies, but again there was a long delay
because of congressional opposition. Roosevelt's decision
taken as commander-in-chief also constituted what by December, 1941, was U.S. involvement in an undeclared limited naval war in the Atlantic.

It is interesting that even the critics of the president's war
powers do not question Roosevelt's judgment of the peril to
national security (probably because they share his liberal values as incorporated in the New Deal and view World War II
as a "good war"). But they do question the constitutional pro-
priety of his actions. Thus, quite typically, Merlo Pusey, after
admitting that had the president gone to Congress he would
have been turned down even though "human freedom was
gravely endangered on a global scale," says: "On grounds of
expediency and of international power politics, the argument
[for the actions Roosevelt took] is very impressive. But where
does it leave us in terms of democratic principles and the
maintenance of constitutional government?"[5] By juxtaposition
of such loaded terms as "expediency" and "power politics"
with "principles" and "democracy," Pusey stacks the odds and
avoids the issue of (1) what Roosevelt should have done and (2)
how to reconcile American democratic government with the
protection of the national security. Pusey dismisses this concern as "one of the inescapable risks in democratic government."[6] The worst, he says, that would have happened had
Roosevelt gone to Congress for support and been rejected
would have been more aggressive behavior by the Nazis on the
assumption that the United States would do nothing to stop
them; they might even have struck the first blow, as Japan
finally did. What Pusey, in sort, argues is that U.S. institutions

could not cope with the critical situation in 1940–41; they could not take the initiative to protect U.S. security, but only react to the enemy's initiatives. But no matter. America's paralysis would have provoked its enemies so that after they had attacked this country Congress could legally have declared war.[7] The integrity of the Constitution in these circumstances could have been preserved. In other words, American democracy, unable to act wisely, would be saved by its enemies' stupidity.

But this avoids the central issue of the effectiveness of American institutions in meeting critical foreign policy situations. What would have happened had the Japanese bypassed Hawaii and had Hitler not declared war on America? Could Roosevelt have organized sufficient congressional and public support to declare war on the Axis powers? It is doubtful, even though by late 1941 Germany had conquered all of Western Europe except England, stood at the gates of Moscow and Leningrad, had captured much of North Africa, and was soon to move within sight of the Suez Canal, while Japan was poised for the conquest of British, French, and Dutch colonies in the Far East with a possible link-up via India with the Germans in the Middle East. In short, but for German and Japanese mistakes, they might have won the war and left the United States, as Roosevelt said in one of his speeches, a lone democratic island in a totalitarian sea, to be dealt with later.

This analysis of the 1940–41 period ought at least to balance the Vietnamese tragedy, for the former is a reminder of the need for presidential initiative and discretion while the latter seems to be a prescription for presidential restraint and congressional supervision. But let us for a moment assume that the War Powers Act had existed before the United States became involved in World War II. In all likelihood, it would have prevented Roosevelt from taking the actions he took. Would Congress have supported the destroyer deal? And would it after sixty days not have opposed the extension of the area of the Atlantic Ocean to be patrolled by U.S. warships, which reported sightings of German ships to the British? Would it not have rejected the president's "shoot-on-sight" order? While Congress did support lend-lease, the key issue was getting the arms across the Atlantic. Ironically, while congressional self-assertion during 1940–41 might well have been extremely detrimental to U.S. interests, the War Powers Act would not have prevented Truman and Johnson from obtaining a declaration of war had they requested one.

CONGRESS, THE VOTERS, AND FOREIGN POLICY

The gist of the arguments presented above is the emphasis on the correctness of the *substantive* content of the policy. The fear is that Congress will act in ways detrimental to the nation's interests. On the other hand, supporters of an increased role in foreign policy decision-making for Congress stress the argument that the United States is, after all, a democracy. Why have a Congress if it is incapable of playing a major role in all areas of policy-making? And, again, so what if Congress occasionally makes a "wrong" decision? Democracy is based on the will of the majority, and who has so much knowledge that he can tell the majority that they are wrong? It is more important, according to this view, for the *method of reaching a decision* to be just than it is for the decision to be "correct" by some criterion (often that of hindsight). Thus, the type of considerations that led to the proposal of a War Powers Act do not depend upon whether Congress makes the "correct" decision on a foreign policy question, but rather on the reestablishment of the proper role of the legislative branch in the decision-making process.

Indeed, one finds support for a stronger role for the Congress in foreign policy decision-making among the members themselves *and* in the general public. A December, 1974 Harris poll found that only 39 percent of the respondents believed that Congress had a "very important role" in the making of foreign policy, behind that of Secretary of State Kissinger (73 percent), the president (43 percent), and business (42 percent). With the exception of public opinion (58 percent), the respondents believed that Congress (49 percent), more than any other individual or institution, should have a stronger role in foreign policy decision-making. A survey of members of the House and the Senate by the General Accounting Office, conducted for the subcommittee on International Political and

Military Affairs of the House International Relations committee, found general dissatisfaction with the quantity, quality,
and timeliness of executive-branch supplied information.[8] The
lone exception occurred in the case of the *Mayaguez*. Yet,
what constitutes a stronger role for Congress in the formulation of foreign policy? Recent events indicate that Congress
has been most assertive in *reacting* to administration decisions
or proposals, but not nearly as successful in initiating foreign
policy alternatives. For example, the Congress did block further aid to the regime in South Vietnam as it became evident
that the long war was finally coming to an end; it did bar funds
for military assistance in Angola; and it did authorize a cutback
in aid to Turkey. Each of these congressional initiatives was
opposed by the administration. Yet, the Congress has made
little effort to enact a comprehensive energy or food policy.
Attempts to restrict the importation of chrome from Rhodesia
and to enact a law which would prohibit American corporations from participating in the Arab boycott of Israel indicated
a potential for a new congressional initiative in foreign policy
decision-making in 1976; yet, the opposition of the Ford Administration to both of these proposals ultimately led to the
result that neither was enacted. On these policies, the independent decision-making capacity of Congress will not be as-
sessed, since the Carter Administration favored both of these
congressional initiatives and these proposals were enacted in
1977. The administration, however, did meet with an early
defeat in Congress, when it was forced to withdraw the nomination of Sorenson to head the CIA. Once again, Congress was
acting negatively rather than initiating any policy; and, furthermore, most observers did not attribute the negative reaction of the Senate to the new president, but rather to the
nominee himself.

Among the reform proposals favored in the General Accounting Office survey were a system in which information
concerning a crisis would automatically flow to the Congress
and a requirement that a senior executive official observe executive deliberations during crises and keep the Congress fully
informed on the international situation. Two proposals were
supported by a narrow margin: (1) granting a small number of
members of Congress observer status on the National Security

Council or other crisis management groups; and (2) establishing direct participation of members in such crisis decision-making organizations. Yet, there was substantial opposition to the establishment of a special congressional committee to serve as a focal point for information during international crises.[9] Thus, even among the representatives and senators themselves, there is not strong support for giving the legislature an important role in actually making the critical decisions on foreign policy. The members want to be informed, but not the immediate responsibility for making the decisions. There are also institutional difficulties which must be realized by those who would increase the role of Congress in foreign policy initiation: New ventures in foreign policy are difficult for large bodies such as the House or the Senate, or even their committees. These legislative bodies, like their counterparts throughout the world, are primarily concerned with domestic policy-making. Unlike the executive branch, they rarely speak with one voice. And, as we have stressed, they often respond slowly to any policy questions, be they domestic or foreign.

If Congress remains the weak link in the federal government, then it does not make much sense to expect representatives and senators to attempt to "convert" the opinions of their constituents into policy positions. The opinion conversion notion of democratic government makes two critical assumptions: (1) representatives reflect the majority sentiment within their constituencies; and (2) a majority of the representatives can act to formulate public policy. But can a majority act? Sometimes it can, but the bulk of the work in Congress is done in committees. There is no direct accountability of these committees to the full House or Senate, although recent reforms have made committee chairmanships less dependent upon the sacrosanct seniority system and more responsive to the members of the majority party. Several chairmen have been deposed in the House, but none so far in the Senate. Yet, except in one instance, every chairman who was overthrown was replaced by the member of the majority party next in line on the seniority ladder. Even the more party-oriented reforms of recent Congresses have not been sufficient to counter the decentralized decision-making system in the legislative branch. The impact that Congress might have on foreign policy has been further weakened by the retirements of Fulbright, chairman of the Senate Foreign Relations committee, and Rep. Thomas Morgan (D., Pa.), head of the House International Relations committee. In each case, the new chairman— John Sparkman (D., Alabama) in the Senate and Clement Zablocki (D., Wisconsin) in the House—was not only less concerned with foreign policy issues than was his predecessor, but was also further away than his predecessor from whatever consensus on these issues existed in the majority party.

If we deny the validity of the second assumption, then it does not seem to matter much whether the first assumption is acceptable. A representative or senator who speaks for his constituency but is powerless to do anything for them is not much of an improvement over a legislator who does not even attempt to determine what the will of his constituency is.

Is there anywhere for a supporter of a stronger congressional role in foreign policy-making to turn? The answer is a tentative "yes." According to another view of democracy, which earlier we called the idea of "popular control of government," the voters select the candidates and parties whose views on the issues are closest to their own. They do not demand that their representative reflect the positions of a majority of his constituents on every issue, but elections are viewed as a check on the positions and administration will adopt. The concept of popular control of government assumes that the positions of the administration can be associated with a particular set of officeholders, particularly the members of Congress of the same party as the president. The opposition party, on the other hand, is associated with a different set of policies. Thus, the voters are offered a choice between competing programs on election day. The voter need not be an "expert" on foreign policy questions. All he would have to know is how he generally reacts to foreign policy issues and which stands each party has taken. Yet the evidence for popular control of government seems no more substantial than did the claims for the opinion conversion notion of representative government. Issues have not played much of a role in elections, and foreign policy issues are even less important than domestic ones. Defenders of the idea of popular control of government maintain that the voters should not be blamed for not expressing themselves on the

issues. The parties, after all, do not offer the voters much of a
choice on the issues, particularly on those dealing with foreign
policy.

Indeed, issue voting is further frustrated by the post-World
War II emphasis on the need for a bipartisan foreign policy. If
foreign policy issues transcend party lines, then how can a
voter express his dissatisfaction with the policies of a given
administration? Until recently, foreign policy votes in Congress have been almost devoid of partisan conflict. The justifi-
cation for a bipartisan foreign policy has been that partisan
conflicts would lead to dramatic shifts in America's relations
with the other nations when one party replaced the other in
power. Yet it is not only the strong points of a nation's foreign
policy—its ability to react quickly to crisis and to pursue consistent policies while maintaining enough flexibility to change
policies when the opportunity and need arise— that continue
from one administration to the next because of a bipartisan
foreign policy. The mistakes of the previous administrations
also follow into succeeding ones. Furthermore, the nation's
policies often become contradictory, as when the United
States tried both to bomb more and to negotiate with the
North Vietnamese, because of the compulsion to seek out a
moderate course which would command bipartisan support.
As James MacGregor Burns has argued:

> The immoderate moderation of American policy, the rigid ad-
> herence to a middle-of-the-road course that is often the most
> dangerous way to travel, stems from a common-sense devotion
> to consensus. And trying once again to follow a middle course
> between falsely conceived extremes proved our undoing.[10]

Critics of bipartisanship in foreign policy decision-making
argue that the nation would not be paralyzed in crisis situations even if partisan debate did occur on international issues.
During a crisis, public opinion and congressional opinion
would undoubtedly rally behind the president as it currently
does. The major difference that a more partisan foreign policy
would produce is that the administration in power would have
to demonstrate to the public that (1) the international event
that provoked a presidential response was indeed a crisis; and

(2) the administration took the appropriate steps in handling the situation. These appear to be the very concerns that supporters of an increased Congressional role have in mind. As Cecil V. Crabb, Jr., has argued, "under bipartisan foreign policy, decisions take on an aura of untouchability." Crabb adds:

> Arguments advanced in behalf of bipartisan foreign policy usually presuppose that by some kind of unexplained process, the government will automatically follow the course best calculated to serve the public interest, if only partisanship can be avoided. . . . Most infrequently is there recognition among supporters of the bipartisan principle that parties, with all their faults, and democratic government are inextricably connected, and that occasional excesses by political parties are part of the price a democracy must pay for the freedom it prizes so highly.

He also maintains that "parties are the most effective mechanism for translating the popular will into governmental policy."[11]

But, if congressional coalitions on foreign policy have been changing in recent years and opposing partisan blocs are becoming prominent in the House of Representatives, it does not seem unreasonable to look at the role of parties in the foreign policy decision-making process. The first question we must pose is, "What would a stronger party system look like?" Then we shall examine the question of how parties *might* become more effective participants in foreign policy decision-making.

PARTY RESPONSIBILITY AND FOREIGN POLICY

In 1950, a special Committee on Political Parties of the American Political Science Association issued a report sharply critical of the American party system. The committee held:

> When there are two parties identifiable by the kinds of action they propose, the voters have an actual choice. On the other hand, the sort of opposition presented by a coalition that cuts across party lines, as a regular thing, tends to deprive the public of a meaningful alternative. When such coalitions are formed

after the elections are over, the public usually finds it difficult to understand the new situation and to reconcile it to the purpose of the ballot. Moreover, on that basis it is next to impossible to hold either party responsible for its political record.[12]

The committee's report contained a clear stand in favor of what is called the "doctrine of responsible party government." To enable the voter to hold a party responsible for the actions of the government, each party should present the electorate with clear-cut programs for executive and legislative action. This is the *programmatic* aspect of party responsibility. Secondly, each party should be ideologically distinct from all other parties in the political system, so that the voters have some basis for making a choice on election day. Finally, each party in the legislature should speak with one voice. If the parties are not internally cohesive in the legislature, the voters have a difficult time deciding exactly whom to hold responsible for the decisions of the government. Instead of conflict between the president and the members of his party in Congress, policy decisions should be reached by the legislative and executive wings of the party jointly. The party out of power, as the "loyal opposition," should not only criticize the victors but also offer alternative programs for legislative action. The arguments advanced in favor of party responsibility thus focus on the basic theme that the party system is the *only* mechanism with the potential to serve as a means of translating the public's will into policy decisions.

The emphasis of the responsible party model is, therefore, not upon "balancing the scales" between the president on the one hand and Congress on the other hand. Indeed, party responsibility requires a solid front on the part of a president and his congressional party. Advocates of party responsibility, however, see as the critical question in foreign policy formation "Do the voters have a set of competing policy alternatives from which to choose?" rather than "Are there competing centers of power within the federal government?" For example, if we consider congressional controversy over the Vietnam War, it is obvious that neither party put forward a specific set of proposals for voter approval or disapproval. Indeed, as Republicans and Democrats in the House of Representatives

were becoming more ideologically distinct and more internally cohesive in their positions on the war, in the Senate a
bipartisan coalition opposing the war was developing. Indeed
the Vietnam experience furnishes perhaps the most dramatic
example of the lack of party responsibility in contemporary
American political history, the election of 1964. Republican
presidential candidate Goldwater openly disagreed with Johnson on the proper course of action the United States should
pursue in Vietnam. Goldwater favored an increased American
role in the war, while Johnson emphatically stated that he
would not send American troops into combat in Vietnam. The
positions of the two candidates were clearly delinated and
each attempted to lead public opinion—as the doctrine of responsible party government prescribes. The Johnson example,
while extreme, is not atypical. In 1968, Nixon ran as an ardent
anti-Communist; in 1972, he reelection campaign rarely failed
to note that he was the first president to establish ties with the
People's Republic of China. During the 1976 race, Carter repeatedly charged Ford with conducting foreign policy without
consulting the American public and pledged to have an
"open" administration. Shortly after taking office in 1977, it
was Carter who complained that too many people (including
members of Congress) had access to sensitive materials on the
conduct of foreign policy—including the names of foreign
chiefs of state who had received money from the CIA.

Indeed, the Carter Administration has vacillated between
the more traditional "closed" foreign policy decision-making
and the openness the new chief executive had promised during the campaign. Both Carter and United Nations ambassador
Andrew Young have shown a propensity to reveal their
thoughts on key international questions to the American public before they have so informed foreign leaders. The Soviets,
among others, have become angered at Carter's frankness on
a new SALT treaty and particularly on the question of human
rights. There have been grumblings about openness even from
our strongest allies in Western Europe, while both Israelis and
Arabs have found cause for alarm in the president's public
statements on what an acceptable Middle East peace settlement should be. To rectify—or "clarify"—the intent of these
public utterances, Carter has sought to reassure other nations

that policy pronouncements he might make are not necessarily binding. But these reassurances take place in closed
meetings, usually private discussions with foreign leaders by
Secretary of State Vance. The foreign press reports worsening
relations with various countries one day and "more progress
than ever" the next. Indeed, Vice-President Mondale has
joked that the United States seems to have a different foreign
policy on different days. Carter himself has admitted that he
talks too much in public (often with inaccurate information)
about foreign policy negotiations. Openness in foreign policy
certainly has its limitations, no matter how great the commitment of an administration to it.

The entire question of responsible party government remains an open one as the nation prepares to enter the 1980s.
Even if the parties do become more ideologically distinct and
programmatic on domestic policy questions, will they do so on
foreign policy issues? Robert Dahl has suggested that such a
change will depend on the politician's "view of reality." And,
in calling for more partisanship on foreign policy issues in
particular, he argued:

> It seems entirely doubtful that it is any longer of much profit to
> a party to avoid taking clear-cut responsibility. Political issues
> are too important to too many voters for ambiguity and evasive-
> ness to pay large dividends today. The parties themselves may
> find it increasingly in their own interest to appear before the
> electorate with a rather well-defined program which, upon elec-
> tion, they will carry through without vast concessions to every
> minor pressure group. Party responsibility seems likely to prove
> profitable to the parties themselves.[13]

In the absence of strong partisan cleavages among the electorate on foreign policy issues, however, it does not seem any
more likely that electoral factors will induce parties to take
more divergent stands on international issues in the 1970s than
they did in the 1950s. There are indeed factors, which we shall
consider below, that might induce the parties to refrain from
being more programmatic on foreign policy issues than on
domestic policies. These obstacles are probably not great
enough to forestall an increase in party responsibility on for-

eign policy issues if a similar increase occurs on domestic policies. Yet the electoral arena is but one stumbling block in the
way of a more responsible party system. We turn now to a
consideration of the various obstacles a party reformer must
face.

THE DILEMMA OF THE PARTY SYSTEM

Even if a more responsible party system were viewed as
desirable by party leaders throughout the country, it would be
a most difficult task to establish such a party system in the
United States. The single greatest obstacle is the fear of the
unknown. When a party has nominated a strong ideologue for
president—such as Goldwater in 1964 for the GOP and
McGovern in 1972 for the Democrats—the result has been
disastrous. Even more critical than the fear of the unknown in
the electoral arena is the fear of the unknown in policy formation. In a system of responsible party government, a change in
party control of the government might mean drastic policy
shifts. If the electorate is fickle, however, and turns incum-
bents out of office with great regularity, then policy formation
would be almost schizophrenic. A law passed by the Democrats might be repealed by the Republicans, only to be rein-
stated when the Democrats came back to power. The
consequences of such a situation would be dramatic for domestic policies; they might be cataclysmic for foreign policies. A
presidential candidate who opposed the detente with mainland China could disrupt American-Chinese relations for
decades. Even if such a president were succeeded by an advocate of better relations between the two countries, the damage
done by his predecessor may effectively block any initiatives
by a new administration. In contrast, a bipartisan foreign policy ensures continued support for the successful policies of the
previous administrations (as well as for the failures). The General Accounting Office survey of congressional attitudes on
legislative-executive relations on foreign policy confirms the
fears of critics of an increased role for political parties. The
study shows substantial differences between Democratic and
Republican members of Congress on how the *Mayaguez* inci-

dent should have been handled, although there are substantial majorities within both congressional parties favoring a more active role for Congress in the future.[14]

But, even if party leaders were no longer to pay lip service to the old shibboleth that a responsible party is doomed to act "irresponsibly" on foreign policy questions, they still must face several critical stumbling blocks in any attempt to make the American parties more programmatic, ideologically distinct, and internally cohesive. Constitutionally, control over party organizations in the United States rests with the individual states, so a recalcitrant member of a congressional party cannot be denied renomination by the national party, as he can in Britain. This electoral base independent of the national party means that there is little a party can do to ensure itself a high level of cohesion in the national legislative branch. Not even a strong and immensely popular president can effectively intervene in the relationship between a member of Congress and his constituents. Franklin D. Roosevelt attempted to translate his 1936 landslide victory into a mandate for his role as party leader in the 1938 congressional elections by asking voters to "purge" disloyal Democratic representatives and senators. The results may have been the biggest political setback Roosevelt ever suffered. The congressional parties are not without any power over recalcitrant members: The party caucuses can strip mavericks of their seniority rights.* Although this method of punishment has been used infrequently, more responsible parties might find it an effective tactic.

An even more difficult constitutional barrier to surmount in the American political system is the relationship between the president and the legislative branch. In a system of responsible party government, legislative-executive relations are marked by cooperation rather than conflict. The chief executive is the leader of his party, and his party controls the government. The government stands or falls on the basis of the public's view of the parties. In the United States, however, the legislative and

*Democrats stripped of seniority for supporting Goldwater in 1964 were Representatives John Bell Williams (Miss.) and Albert Watson (S.C.). Watson immediately resigned his House seat and won reelection as a Republican. In 1969, House Democrats stripped Representative John Rarick (La.) of his seniority rights for supporting American Independent candidate George C. Wallace in the 1968 presidential contest.

executive branches are separate and supposedly equal according to the Constitution. Because the president is elected every four years, the members of the House every two years, and senators every six years, it is not unusual for one party to win the presidency but not majorities in each house of Congress. From 1947 to 1978, one or the other party controlled both the legislative and executive branches for only 14 years—less than half of the time.* When control of the two major branches of the government is divided, domestic policy-making must either involve major concessions by both parties (as occurred under Eisenhower) or virtually grind to a halt (as happened under Truman and Nixon). In neither case is there any room for party responsibility. Indeed, in the area of foreign policy, divided control of the government creates a power vacuum that enhances presidential dominance in the policy-making role.

The separation of powers in the American political system may thus function as the strongest barrier to a more responsible party system in the United States. In contrast, a parliamentary system such as is found in England and many West European nations makes responsible parties more feasible. The prime minister is not elected by the people at large but is chosen by the party (or a coalition of parties) that wins the most seats in the legislature. Divided control of the legislative and executive branches of government is therefore impossible. Furthermore, the prime minister, unlike the president, must tailor his policies to the wishes of his Parliamentary party. If he refuses to do so, he can conceivably be removed from office by the Parliament—or pressured into resigning. A major failure on a policy decision can result in the formation of a new government. Anthony Eden was replaced as prime minister of Britain in 1956 by Harold Macmillan after a major foreign policy blunder in the Middle East. Eden had committed Brit-

*The American voters have been remarkably consistent in returning majorities to the House and the Senate of the same party. Voters returned bare majorities of Republicans (by two in the House, one in the Senate) to Congress in the election of 1930; by the time Congress had actually convened, several Republican deaths allowed the Democrats to organize the House. Not since the adoption of direct election of Senators have voters actually split control of the two houses of Congress between the two parties.

ish troops during the Egyptian-Israeli war to a joint effort with
the French to recapture control of the Suez Canal from the
Egyptians, who had seized control of the waterway. The Brit-
ish-French attempt failed and Eden resigned. In the United
States, on the other hand, Woodrow Wilson argued that

> . . . our system is essentially astronomical. A president's useful-
> ness is measured, not by efficiency, but by calendar months. It
> is reckoned that if he be good at all, he will be good for four
> years. A prime minister must keep himself in favor with the
> majority, a president need only keep alive.[15]

American Presidents can afford to take actions that risk failure early in their administrations. Because they have as long
as three and a half years to recover from their "mistakes," they
are virtually unchecked. Even the 1973 vote against Nixon's
policies in Cambodia could hardly be taken as a guarantee that
the administration's basic foreign policy objectives in Southeast Asia would be altered significantly. In contrast to the
American presidents, who can define situations as "crises" almost at will, a prime minister may find that his very tenure in
office is dependent upon the foreign policy risks he chooses to
take. Unless he is quite certain the the Parliament will support
his actions, a prime minister is unlikely to engage in foreign
policy adventures that do not directly involve the defense of
his own nation.

In summary, the electoral obstacles to a more responsible
party system do not appear to be as critical in the 1970s as they
were in earlier years. If voters are becoming more polarized
on domestic policies than in previous years—*and if the parties
respond to the cleavages in the electorate*—then foreign policy
issues are virtually bound to become more entangled in the
debates over domestic politics and national priorities. Indeed,
there is some indication that congressional parties are becoming more distinct on foreign policy questions. Furthermore, as
policies which formerly were viewed as purely domestic
become "intermestic," the traditional partisan divisions on domestic issues are likely to be found on foreign policy questions
as well. Yet the barriers to responsible party government established in the constitutional provisions of separation of pow-

ers and the fixed four-year term of the president (and such additional barriers as the requirement that treaties receive the approval of two-thirds of the Senate) appear virtually insurmountable. Where are we to turn?

THE PRESIDENT PROPOSES, THE CONGRESS REACTS?

Perhaps there is a lesser, if not minor, role that Congress can still play in foreign policy decision-making even if it does not involve anything like equality with the president. Such a role would stress the "oversight" function of Congress, in which the legislative branch investigates the procedures and policies of the executive, makes recommendations for future policy, and even sets guidelines which must be followed. Samuel P. Huntington has argued that Congress is incapable of formulating policy (domestic or foreign) and recommends that it devote most of its resources to oversight.[16] Indeed, the Legislative Reorganization Act of 1970, one of the recent congressional reforms, mandated increased oversight for all committees in the Congress. What are the prospects for oversight and how well can such a function satisfy the critics who insist upon a stronger role on foreign policy for the legislature?

The prospects for oversight can perhaps best be summed up by the traditional refrain: The word "oversight" has two meanings and, in the Congress, there has been an overemphasis on the meaning *not* intended by those who want more of a balance of power in the national government. The difficulty is that in too many cases, the regulators (congressional investigators) become the accomplices of the groups or organizations they are supposed to investigate and control.[17] Furthermore, as Morris Ogul argues, the oversight function is not terribly salient to most members of Congress.[18] Even when members do become concerned with their oversight duties, the close working relationships that develop among the legislators, bureaucrats, and interest groups ("those cozy triangles"[19]) are not conducive to critical examinations of the behavior of each other. A staff member of the House Armed Services committee stated the case simply: "Our committee is a real estate committee."[20]

Yet, there has been an increase in critical oversight in recent years. In particular, both the House and the Senate established oversight committees to investigate the abuses of power of the Central Intelligence Agency and the Federal Bureau of Investigation in the 94th Congress (1975–76). Yet, the very fact that such committees were established points to one of the weaknesses in the congressional oversight procedure. Institutional loyalties prevailed, so that no thought was given to a joint committee—which would have saved duplication of effort. In each house, a select committee (as opposed to one of the more traditional standing committees) was formed for the investigations. Yet, there existed committees on foreign relations, armed services, government operations, and judiciary (in the case of the FBI) in each house which could just as effectively have conducted the oversight. Why were select committees employed, then? Again, the question of institutional loyalties arose within congressional committees, and there was also a problem of where the ultimate jurisdiction is to be placed.

Once established, the Intelligence committees did not function smoothly. In the Senate, many critics claimed that chairman Frank Church was headline hunting and was trying to conclude the hearings as quickly as possible to allow him to enter the Democratic presidential primaries. The Pike committee in the House drew better "press notices," but the lower house produced a spectacle of its own. The original House Intelligence Committee was chaired by Rep. Lucien Nedzi (D., Mich.). A conflict within the committee developed when maverick Rep. Michael Harrington (D., Mass.) "leaked" to the press classified material on the CIA's role in "destabilizing" the Allende government in Chile in 1973. Nedzi demanded that Harrington be removed from the committee, and there was a movement within the House to censure Harrington. The Harrington case was overshadowed by further leaks to the press and the entire matter was finally closed on a rather obscure technicality that saved Harrington from possible action by his fellow House members. Speaker Carl Albert finally resolved the dispute between supporters of Nedzi and those of Harrington by reconstituting the committee without either member. Like its Senate counterpart, the House Intelligence committee was established as a permanent committee in 1977.

What did the Intelligence committees accomplish? They did bring to public attention a large number of abuses of power by the FBI and particularly by the CIA. Yet, much of this publicity arose through leaks and much of what we learned about the intelligence agencies came from newspapers and magazine follow-up stories rather than from congressional testimony. Indeed, Pike and Ford were at loggerheads on what the committee could or could not release. The full House ultimately sided with the president against a moderate Democrat. Much of the impetus for reform was slowed when Richard Welch, a CIA operative in Greece, was assassinated. Many people thought that the congressional hearings were divulging too much information about the agency, thereby making the intelligence operations of the United States vulnerable throughout the world. Ultimately, the Congress did take some action: It forbade the CIA from engaging in domestic intelligence operations and it also passed a law which made the assassination of foreign leaders illegal—an action that would make few foreign chiefs of state sleep more soundly at night. Attempts to make the CIA budget available to at least the relevant congressional personnel failed. No wide-ranging reorientation of foreign intelligence was mandated by the Congress. The decision in 1977 to place all intelligence operations dealing with foreign policy under a single agency, headed by CIA Director Turner, was made in the White House, not on Capital Hill.

Congressional oversight on foreign policy has not been totally ineffective. Congress did interrogate Kissinger to a greater extent than during any other recent period on the details of the 1975 Sinai accord. As discussed above, Congress has passed, over Nixon's veto, a War Powers Act; and, against the wishes of the Nixon Administration, the legislature required the secretary of state to submit the final text of any executive agreement on foreign policy to Congress within 60 days. Yet, oversight does not seem to have strengthened the role of Congress in terms of implementing policy. Oversight has all of the advantages of hindsight, but requires considerably more effort. Those who want to strengthen the role of Congress in determining what the foreign policy of the United States *will be*, as opposed to what it should have been, will demand a more important function for the legislature. But, that brings us full circle to a reconsideration of how powerful the legislative and executive branches of government should be.

THE DEMOCRATIC DILEMMA RECONSIDERED

We have seen that one way of resolving the problem of how much power each branch of the government should have on foreign policy, strengthening the power of Congress, can at least in part be accomplished by "reforms" such as the War Powers Act or increased oversight. But, this will not necessarily lead to further congressional *control* over foreign policy decisions. On the other hand, a change that would give Congress more power on foreign policy, strengthening political parties to the point of sharing responsibility with the executive, might not be possible to initiate.

Is there an answer to the problem of foreign policy decision-making in a democracy? Probably not, if one insists upon a panacea for the failures in foreign policy and a guarantee that successful policies will continue to be chosen. The decision-making process on foreign policy questions appears to work best in crisis situations, when immediate and decisive action is required. Perhaps leaders function best in crises—or perhaps the "followers" are simply more likely to support the leaders. The decision-making process works less well in such protracted conflicts as the wars in Vietnam and Korea, where the objectives are more limited and the stakes are lower. On program policies, the system appears to be least effective. Stated most simply, a democratic political system appears to handle foreign policy decisions best when the fewest actors—the inner circle—are involved in the process of decision-making. As more and more actors in all four circles become involved, the conflict between presidential formation of foreign policy and the desires of other actors to have a say in foreign policy becomes intense. In crisis decision-making, the administration chooses a course of action designed to maximize a given goal. The decision that is reached is directly related to that goal. Students of the foreign policy-making process have praised the decisions made in crises and concluded that democratic governments can indeed rival monolithic dictatorships in response to external threats, citing the pattern of rational decision-making in such situations as the reason why the American political system has fared so well in crises. Lowi has stated that

> ... *crisis decisions in foreign policy are made by an elite of formal, official office-holders.* Rarely is there time to go further ... the people who make decisions in times of crisis are largely those who were elected and appointed to make such decisions. That is to say, *in foreign affairs crises our government has operated pretty much as it was supposed to operate.* There is a normative corollary as well: Since our record of response to crisis is good, then the men in official positions have been acting and are able to act rationally. ... Indeed, a fundamental feature of crisis decisions is that they involve institution leaders (holders of the top posts) *without their institutions.* Only when time allows does the entire apparatus of the foreign policy establishment come in play.[21]

On program policies, however, the decisions reached through bureaucratic politics are often "minimal" ones; they do not resolve issues one way or the other and often cannot be justified on the basis that they maximize any particular foreign policy goal. Indeed, it is possible that bureaucratic politics may lead to no decisions at all—if the contending forces are each strong enough and obstinate enough to prevent a compromise acceptable to all (or even most) parties.

In addition, in program policies—and limited wars—the objectives of the policy as well as as the proposed ways of handling them often lack the clarity of crisis decision-making.* In Vietnam, for example, the objectives of American policy were never clearly delineated. On the one hand, a policy of total war was never seriously considered by the Johnson or Nixon Administration. However, neither was the policy of withdrawal of

---

*Limited wars are much like program policies in that both types of foreign policy decisions (1) involve multiple actors; (2) take a considerable amount of time to reach a conclusion; (3) involve conflicting goals on what a policy is supposed to accomplish; (4) involve bargaining—generally among the combatants rather than domestically—and are ultimately resolved by a negotiated settlement; and (5) are often marked by minimal decisions.

all American troops, and both administrations flatly rejected what might appear to have been a "rational" compromise first suggested by other nations and then advocated by North Vietnam: a coalition government in South Vietnam. The result was a set of minimal decisions: to increase American troop strength during the Johnson Administration, but to continue to press for a negotiated settlement to the conflict. By contrast, Nixon reduced American troop strength but increased the bombing of North Vienam, again continuing to search for a negotiated settlement. Yet the strategies of both administrations involved contradictory policies, producing what Burns has called an "immoderate moderation." The United States finally extricated itself from the war without ever having resolved the question of what goals were accomplished by the many years of costly fighting.

If it is then concluded that decision-making works best— produces the "best" results or garners the most public support —in crisis situations, we must, in conclusion, address ourselves again to the democratic dilemma posed at the beginning of the study. To ensure its security in the essentially anarchical international system, a state must have a concentration of executive authority so that it can respond quickly and with unity of purpose to events in the international political system. A democratic state, on the other hand, requires a restraint on executive power to preserve the constitutional system. This tension between the needs of international and domestic systems spills over into the distinction between crisis decision-making and program policies. Decision-making in crisis situations very much resembles authoritarian decision-making: Policies are determined by a relatively small number of actors who must act with dispatch and unity. Democratic politics, on the other hand, is often marked by the necessity to compromise, to consider issues at great length in the attempt to reconcile conflicting interests, and to highlight the different goals of the actors involved rather than to assume that the decision-makers all agree upon the goals to be maximized.

The irony of foreign policy decision-making is thus that the American political system appears to function best when decisions are made in the very way authoritarian states formulate policies.[22] When foreign policy decisions become more

"democratic" by encompassing more actors, the policies selected may not have as clear a relationship to the strategic
problem at hand. The democratic dilemma does not admit of
a ready answer. The framers of the Constitution did indeed
produce a document with "missing powers," allowing for the
growth of presidential power to meet changing needs. And by
consciously creating a form of government that was inimical to
responsible party government,[23] the framers of the Constitution ensured that the legislative branch could not take the
foreign policy initiative away from the executive—an initiative
they had given him. Believing that the nation would engage
in no "entangling alliances," against which George Washington was to admonish the country in his Farewell Address, the
Founding Fathers expected the war-making powers given to
Congress in the Constitution would provide an adequate
check on Presidential dominance of the foreign policy process.

The President will, however, remain the dominant actor in
foreign policy decision-making. The conduct of an activist foreign policy—as distinct from a neo-isolationist one—will continue to require a strong foreign policy president. Thus, the
basic dilemma remains: What is a virtue internationally may be
a vice domestically, and what is a virtue domestically—a restraint on executive power—may become a vice internationally. The basic question is whether the United States can grant
its government sufficient authority to safeguard the nation
while yet preserving its democratic system. The purpose of
America's foreign policy, in the final analysis, is to protect its
democratic way of life. Yet, will the policy subvert the very
purposes it was intended to serve?

The profound effects that the war in Vietnam had on the
relationship between the president and Congress and, indeed,
even on the party system will probably serve to restrain future
chief executives in foreign policy somewhat. Whether Johnson's personal popularity declined because of the Vietnam situation or because of domestic unrest, it is certain that his place
in history will be marred by Vietnam; presumably no future
president will wish to repeat this experience. Nor is it probable
that presidents will be quite so willing to seek out direct confrontations with Congress after Nixon's suprising defeat on the
Cambodian and war powers issues in 1973 and the refusal of

Congress to authorize funds for Ford's requests on Vietnam and Angola. These acts do not, however, mean that Congress will continue to assert itself on foreign policy. The Democratic party in the House of Representatives, through its caucus, had gone on record as opposing further aid to Vietnam in 1971, 1973, and 1975. The caucus action, however, did not result in legislative action until 1975, by which time the Vietnamese government in the south had virtually fallen and public support for continued American aid had virtually evaporated. For Congress, and particularly the congressional parties, to take a stronger role in policy formation, the members would have to translate their policy pronouncements in committees, caucuses, and particularly subcommittees into legislative action which is supported in both the House and the Senate. This is no small task indeed.

The country will continue to rally around the president in crisis situations, although he will probably be less prone to treat foreign policy decisions as critical international events. In short, if future administrations work toward reaching a detente with Russia and rapprochement with China in the international system, the role of the president will shift in emphasis from commander-in-chief to chief diplomat. How long the lessons of Vietnam will be remembered is impossible to predict. World War I was the "war to end all wars." The ending of World War II by the detonation of atomic weapons was supposed to underline the dangers of any future international conflict. General Douglas MacArthur, commenting on the Korean War, stated that it was sheer folly for the United States to fight a land war in Asia; but that did not prevent Vietnam. As George Santayana noted, any nation that doesn't learn from history is doomed to repeat it. The question is: Which lesson should it learn—the lesson of 1940–41 or that of Vietnam?

NOTES

CHAPTER 1

1. Aaron Wildavsky, "The Two Presidencies," *Trans-Action* (December, 1966), p. 7.
2. Paul Seabury, in *Power, Freedom and Diplomacy* (New York: Vintage Books, 1967), p. 189, elaborates on this tension.
3. John Locke, *Two Treatises of Government* (Cambridge: Cambridge University Press, 1960), pp. 383–84 (italics and capitalization of nouns omitted).
4. Seabury, *Power, Freedom and Diplomacy,* p. 196.
5. Richard Neustadt and Graham Allison, in the afterword to Robert F. Kennedy, *The Thirteen Days* (New York: W. W. Norton, 1971), p. 142.
6. Ivor W. Jennings, *Cabinet Government* (Cambridge: Cambridge University Press, 1951), p. 183.
7. Seabury, *Power, Freedom and Diplomacy,* p. 196.
8. Louis Henkin, *Foreign Affairs and the Constitution* (Mineola, N.Y.: The Foundation Press), p. 37.
9. *Ibid.,* p. 41.
10. J. William Fulbright, *The Crippled Giant* (New York: Random House, Vintage Books, 1972), p. 241.
11. Roger Hilsman, *To Move a Nation* (New York: Doubleday, 1967), p. 541.
12. See Stephen D. Krasner, "Are Bureaucracies Important?" *Foreign Policy* (Summer, 1972), pp. 159–79, for an incisive critique of the bureaucratic model.
13. *Ibid.,* p. 168.
14. See Kenneth N. Waltz, *Foreign Policy and Democratic Politics* (Boston: Little, Brown, 1967), pp. 274–75, and John E. Mueller, *War, Presidents, and Public Opinion* (New York: John Wiley, 1973), p. 211.

15. Robert H. Salisbury, "The Analysis of Public Policy: A Search for Theo-
    ries and Roles," in Austin Ranney, ed., *Political Science and Public
    Policy* (Chicago: Markham, 1968), p. 158. See also Salisbury and John
    Heinz, "A Theory of Policy Analysis and Some Preliminary Applica-
    tions," in Ira Sharkansky, ed., *Policy Analysis and Political Science*
    (Chicago: Markham, 1970), pp. 39–60.

    On the original distinction between distributive and redistributive
    policies in the literature of political science, see the pioneering article
    by Theodore J. Lowi, "American Business, Public Policy, Case Studies,
    and Political Theory," *World Politics* (July, 1964), pp. 677–715. On the
    applicability of distributive and redistributive policies to the study of
    foreign policy, see James N. Rosenau, "Foreign Policy as an Issue Area,"
    in Rosenau, ed., *Domestic Sources of Foreign Policy* (New York: The
    Free Press, 1967), pp. 11–50; and Lowi, "Making Democracy Safe for the
    World: National Politics and Foreign Policy," in *ibid.*, pp. 295–331.
16. Wildavsky, "Two Presidencies," pp. 7–8.
17. Bayless Manning, "The Congress, the Executive and Intermestic Affairs:
    Three Proposals," *Foreign Affairs*, January, 1977, pp. 306–24.

CHAPTER 2

1. *New York Times*, January 21, 1961.
2. Wildavsky, "Two Presidencies" (n. 1, Chapter 1), p. 8.
3. John F. Campbell, *The Foreign Affairs Fudge Factory* (New York, Basic
   Books, 1971), pp. 18–19.
4. Adam Yarmolinsky, *The Military Establishment* (New York: Harper &
   Row, 1971), p. 19.
5. Quoted by Robert A. Dahl, *Congress and Foreign Policy* (New York:
   Harcourt Brace Jovanovich, 1950), pp. 129–30.
6. Joseph Jones, *The Fifteen Weeks* (New York: Viking Press, 1955), pp.
   138–41.
7. Arthur M. Schlesinger, Jr., *The Bitter Heritage*, p. 47.
8. Fulbright, *Crippled Giant* (n. 10, Chapter 1), pp. 218–20; and *The Pentagon Papers* (New York: Bantam Books, 1971), p. 25.
9. *Pentagon Papers*, p. 79.
10. Arthur M. Schlesinger, Jr., "Congress and the Making of American For-
    eign Policy," *Foreign Affairs* (October, 1972), p. 98.
11. Quoted by Joseph C. Goulden, *Truth Is the First Casualty* (Chicago:
    Rand McNally, 1969), pp. 50–55. See also Eugene G. Windchy, *Tonkin
    Gulf* (New York: Doubleday, 1971).
12. See, for example, David Halberstam, *The Best and the Brightest* (New
    York: Random House, 1972).
13. John W. Spanier, *The Truman-MacArthur Controversy and the Korean
    War*, rev. ed. (New York: W. W. Norton, 1965).

14. Fulbright, *Crippled Giant,* pp. 188–91.
15. Thomas F. Eagleton, "Whose Power is War Power?" *Foreign Policy* (Fall, 1972), pp. 29–31.
16. Jacob Javits in *New York Times,* February 14, 1972. See also Javits, *Who Makes War: The President Versus Congress* (New York: William Morrow, 1973).

CHAPTER 3

1. Roger Hilsman, *The Politics of Policy-Making in Defense and Foreign Affairs* (New York: Harper & Row, 1971), pp. 118–20.
2. Mueller, *War, Presidents, and Public Opinion* (n. 15, Chapter 1), p. 169.
3. Morton H. Halperin and Arnold Kanter call these roles "players" and "organizational participants" in "The Bureaucratic Perspective: A Preliminary Framework," in Halperin and Kanter, eds., *Readings in American Foreign Policy* (Boston: Little, Brown, 1973), pp. 9–10.
4. Yet, as Halberstam noted in *Best and Brightest* (n. 12, Chapter 2), academics like McGeorge Bundy and Rostow quickly became "operators" and lost their independent perspective.
5. Hilsman, *To Move a Nation* (n. 11, Chapter 1), pp. 571–72.
6. Hilsman, *Politics of Policy-Making,* pp. 119–20.
7. Henry T. Nash, *American Foreign Policy: Response to a Sense of Threat* (Homewood, Ill.: Dorsey, 1973), p. 99.
8. *Ibid.,* p. 95.
9. Henry A., Kissinger, "Bureaucracy and Policy-Making: The Effects of Insiders and Outsiders on the Policy Process," in Halperin and Kanter, eds., *Readings in American Foreign Policy,* p. 89.
10. Francis E. Rourke, *Bureaucracy and Foreign Policy* (Baltimore: Johns Hopkins University Press, 1973), p. 32.
11. *Ibid.,* p. 30.
12. See David E. Price, *Who Makes the Laws?* (Morristown, N. J.: General Learning Press, 1972).
13. Melvin Gurtov, *The First Vietnam Crisis* (New York: Columbia University Press, 1967).
14. Arthur H. Vandenberg, ed., *The Private Papers of Senator Vandenberg* (Boston: Houghton Mifflin, 1952), pp. 342–44.
15. Samuel P. Huntington, *The Common Defense* (New York: Columbia University Press, 1961), pp. 130–31.
16. In the House, there are 45 members of the Appropriations committee, 40 members of Armed Services, and 25 members of the Budget committee. For these 110 positions, there are 109 members (one member of Budget also serves on Armed Services). In the Senate, Appropriations has 25 members, Armed Services has 18, and Budget has 16. These 59 positions are filled by 57 individuals (more than half of the entire Sen-

ate!), with one member of Armed Services on Appropriations and another on Budget.

17. See Roger H. Davidson and Walter Oleszek, *Congress Against Itself* (Bloomington: Indiana University Press, 1977). On reforms that were adopted, see Leroy N. Rieselbach, *Congressional Reform in the Seventies* (Morristown, N.J.: General Learning Press, 1977).

18. Arnold Kanter, "Congress and the Defense Budget: 1960–1970," *American Political Science Review* (March, 1972), p. 132.

19. Eric M. Uslaner, "Conditions for Party Responsibility: Partisanship in the House of Representatives, 1947–1970" (unpublished Ph.D. dissertation, Indiana University, 1973), Chapter 6.

20. Eric M. Uslaner, "Cyclical and Secular Models of Congressional Voting," (University of Maryland, College Park, mimeo, 1977).

21. *Ibid.*

22. *Ibid.*

23. Ernest A. Gross, "What Is a Bipartisan Foreign Policy?" *Department of State Bulletin* (October 3, 1949), pp. 504–5.

24. For data on the 1940's and 1950's, see Leroy N. Rieselbach, *The Roots of Isolationism* (Indianapolis: Bobbs-Merrill, 1966), esp. p. 52. More recent findings are in Uslaner, "Conditions for Party Responsibility," Chapters 5 and 6.

25. Lester W. Milbrath, *The Washington Lobbyists* (Chicago: Rand McNally, 1963), pp. 162–64.

26. Lester W. Milbrath, "Interest Groups and Foreign Policy," in Rosenau, ed., *Domestic Sources*, p. 241.

27. Raymond A. Bauer, Ithiel de Sola Pool, and Lewis Anthony Dexter, *American Business and Public Policy*, 2d ed. (Chicago: Aldine-Atherton, 1972), pp. 300–1.

28. *Ibid.*, p. 398.

29. Wildavsky, "Two Presidencies."

30. Huntington, *Common Defense*, p. 216.

31. Barry S. Rundquist, "The House Seniority System and the Distribution of Prime Military Contracts," paper presented at the 1971 Annual Meeting of the American Political Science Association, pp. 20–21.

32. See Bruce M. Russett, *What Price Vigilance?* (New Haven: Yale University Press, 1970); Stephen A. Cobb, "Defense Spending and Foreign Policy in the House of Representatives," *Journal of Conflict Resolution* (September, 1969), pp. 358–69; and *idem*, "The United States Senate and the Impact of Defense Spending Concentrations" (unpublished ms., Tennessee State University), 1972.

33. See Bernard C. Cohen, *The Public's Impact on Foreign Policy* (Boston: Little, Brown, 1973), pp. 96–97.

34. *Ibid.*, p. 104.

35. For a combination of these two viewpoints, see Richard J. Barnet, *The Roots of War* (Baltimore: Penguin Books, 1973). Among others of this genre, see Sidney Lens, *The Military-Industrial Complex* (Philadelphia: Pilgrim Press, 1970); Ralph Lapp, *The Weapons Culture* (Baltimore:

Penguin Books, 1969); and, perhaps the most balanced one, Yarmolinsky, *Military Establishment* (n. 4, Chapter 2).

36. Detailed analysis of American imperialism may be found in, among other books, Carl Oglesby and Richard Shaull, *Containment and Change* (New York: Macmillan, 1967), and in any of the several volumes by Gabriel Kolko on U.S. foreign policy during World War II and since; a briefer statement of Kolko's view is presented in *The Roots of American Foreign Policy* (Boston: Beacon Press, 1969).

37. Cohen, *Public's Impact on Foreign Policy,* pp. 98–104.

38. See Waltz, *Foreign Policy and Democratic Politics,* pp. 274–75; and Mueller, *War, Presidents, and Public Opinion,* p. 211 (both n. 15, Chapter 1).

39. Rosenau, "Foreign Policy as an Issue Area," pp. 24–36.

40. Gabriel Almond, *The American People and Foreign Policy* (New York: Praeger, 1960), p. 232.

41. *Ibid.,* p. 54.

42. Francis E. Rourke, "The Domestic Scene," in Robert E. Osgood, ed., *America and the World* (Baltimore: Johns Hopkins Press, 1970), pp. 149–62. See also "The Domestic Scene: The President's Ascendent," pp. 82–88, and Robert E. Tucker, "The American Outlook: Change and Continuity," pp. 33–38, in Osgood, ed., *Retreat from Empire?* (Baltimore: Johns Hopkins Press, 1973).

43. Mueller, *War, Presidents, and Public Opinion,* p. 53.

44. *Ibid.;* for a more detailed analysis, somewhat at odds with Mueller's reasoning for this loss of presidential (especially Johnson's) support, see Lawrence Elowitz, "The American Political System and Limited War" (unpublished Ph.D. dissertation, University of Florida, 1972).

45. This conclusion is drawn from Table 3.4 of Mueller, *War, Presidents, and Public Opinion,* p. 61. Mueller does not draw his inference himself, but the regression coefficients in the table for opposition to the war do support the claim.

46. *Ibid.,* pp. 54–55.

47. *Ibid.,* p. 50.

48. A good statement of this position is found in Austin Ranney and Willmoore Kendall, *Democracy and the American Party System* (New York: Harcourt Brace Jovanovich, 1956), Chapter 4.

49. See Hanna Fenichel Pitkin, *The Concept of Representation* (Berkeley: University of California Press, 1967), Chapter 4.

50. Warren E. Miller, "Voting and Foreign Policy," in Rosenau, *Domestic Sources,* pp. 215–26; and Mueller, *War, Presidents, and Public Opinion,* p. 227.

51. Miller, "Voting and Foreign Policy," p. 229.

52. The five domestic issue areas studies were federal aid to education, medical care, federal job guarantee, fair employment legislation, and school integration. See Gerald M. Pomper, "From Confusion to Clarity: Issues and American Voters, 1956–1968," *American Political Science Review* (June, 1972), pp. 415–29.

53. See Richard W. Boyd, "Popular Control of Public Policy: A Normal Vote Analysis of the 1968 Election," *American Political Science Review* (June, 1972), pp. 429–46.

54. See Benjamin I. Page and Richard A. Brody, "Policy Voting and the Electoral Process: The Vietnam War Issue," *American Political Science Review* (September, 1972), p. 983.

55. *Ibid.*, p. 983, n. 18.

56. Boyd, "Popular Control," Table 2, p. 433.

57. For evidence of a relationship, see Elowitz, "Political System and Limited War." For evidence of no relationship, see Mueller, *War, Presidents, and Public Opinion,* p. 227.

58. Warren E. Miller and Donald E. Stokes, "Constituency Influence in Congress," *American Political Science Review* (March, 1963), pp. 45–56; and Miller, "Majority Rule and the Representative System," paper presented at the 1962 Annual Meeting of the American Political Science Association.

59. The findings of Miller and Stokes and those of Miller are summarized in Leroy N. Rieselbach, *Congressional Politics* (New York: McGraw-Hill, 1973), p. 333.

60. Richard F. Fenno, *Congressmen in Committees* (Boston: Little, Brown, 1973), pp. 5–14.

61. John Dewey, *The Public and its Problems* (Denver: Swallow Press, n.d.), p. 116.

CHAPTER 4

1. Thomas C. Schelling, *Arms and Influence* (New Haven: Yale University Press, 1966).

2. Henry A. Kissinger, *Nuclear Weapons and Foreign Policy* (New York: Harper & Row, 1957).

3. See Anthony Downs, *An Economic Theory of Democracy* (New York: Harper & Row, 1957), among others.

4. Most prominently, see Hans J. Morgenthau, *Politics Among Nations,* 4th ed. (New York: Alfred A. Knopf, 1967), esp. pp. 5–8.

5. See, in particular, Charles E. Lindblom, *The Intelligence of Democracy* (New York: Free Press, 1965), and Richard F. Fenno, Jr., *The Power of the Purse* (Boston: Little, Brown, 1966).

6. Lindblom, *Intelligence of Democracy,* pp. 98 ff.

7. *Ibid.*, p. 99.

8. Graham T. Allison, "Conceptual Models and the Cuban Missile Crisis," *American Political Science Review* (September, 1969), p. 716.

9. I. M. Destler, *Presidents, Bureaucrats, and Foreign Policy* (Princeton, N. J.: Princeton University Press, 1972), pp. 52 ff and 118 ff.

10. Oran R. Young, *The Politics of Force* (Princeton, N.J.: Princeton Univer-

sity Press, 1968), pp. 6–15, and Charles F. Hermann, ed., *International Crises* (New York: Free Press, 1972).

11. For the Cuban missile crisis, see Elie Abel, *The Missile Crisis* (New York: Bantam Books, 1966); Alexander L. George *et al.*, eds., *The Limits of Coercive Diplomacy* (Boston: Little, Brown, 1971), pp. 86–143; and Kennedy, *Thirteen Days* (n. 5, Chapter 1).

12. Rourke, "Domestic Scene," in Osgood, *Retreat from Empire?* (n. 41. Chapter 3), pp. 88–89.

13. The Nixon decision has been reconstructed from the *New York Times* of the period and Henry Brandon, *The Retreat of American Power* (Garden City, N.Y.: Doubleday, 1973).

14. Halperin and Kanter, "Bureaucratic Perspective" (n. 3, Chapter 3), pp. 9–10.

15. Quoted by Alexander L. George, "Making Foreign Policy," *American Political Science Review* (September, 1972), p. 754.

16. Warner R. Schilling, "The H-Bomb Decision: How to Decide without Actually Choosing," in Halperin and Kanter, eds., *Readings in American Foreign Policy* (n. 3, Chapter 3), p. 255.

17. Morton H. Halperin, "The Decision to Deploy the ABM: Bureaucratic and Domestic Politics in the Johnson Administration," *World Politics* (October, 1972), p. 83. On decision-making on the ABM, also see Halperin, *Bureaucratic Politics and Foreign Policy* (Washington: Brookings Institution, 1974); and Alton Frye, *A Responsible Congress: The Politics of National Security* (New York: McGraw-Hill, 1975), esp. Chapter 2.

18. *Ibid.*, p. 74.

19. *Ibid.*, pp. 67–69.

20. *Ibid.*, p. 69.

21. *Ibid.*, p. 76.

22. Hilsman, *To Move a Nation*, p. 546.

23. Halperin, "Decision to Deploy," p. 87.

24. Robert S. McNamara, "The Dynamics of Nuclear Strategy," *Department of State Bulletin* (October 9, 1967), pp. 443–51.

25. Abram Chayes and Jerome B. Wiesner, eds., *ABM: An Evaluation of the Decision to Deploy an Antiballistic Missile System* (New York: Harper & Row, 1969), pp. 259–64. Nixon's speech is reproduced on pp. 254–59.

26. Informal discussions with several congressmen provide the basis for this claim.

27. See Eric M. Uslaner, "Congressional Attitudes and Congressional Behavior: The House Decision on the ABM," paper presented at the 1973 Annual Meeting of the Midwest Political Science Association.

28. George H. Gallup, *The Gallup Poll: Public Opinion 1935–1971* (New York: Random House, 1972), vol. 3, pp. 2181 and 2190.

29. Uslaner, "Congressional Attitudes."

30. E. E. Schattschneider, *The Semi-Sovereign People* (New York: Holt, Rinehart and Winston, 1960).

31. Charles O. Jones, *Clear Air* (Pittsburgh: University of Pittsburgh Press, 1975).

CHAPTER 5

1. *New York Times,* January 14, 1973.
2. "Will the Real Senate Stand Up?" *Christian Science Monitor,* May 29–June 1, 1970.
3. For a discussion of some of these reforms, notably the "subcommittee bill of rights," see Leroy N. Rieselbach, *Congressional Reform in the Seventies* (Morristown, N.J.: General Learning Press, 1977).
4. Robert A. Divine, *The Reluctant Belligerent* (New York: John Wiley, 1965); and *idem, Roosevelt and World War II* (Baltimore: Penguin Books, 1969).
5. Merlo J. Pusey, *The Way We Go to War* (Boston: Houghton Mifflin, 1971), p. 74.
6. *Ibid.,* p. 75.
7. *Ibid.*
8. Report of the Comptroller General of the United States, *Executive-Legislative Communications and the Role of the Congress During International Crises* (Washington: General Accounting Office, 1976).
9. *Ibid.,* pp. iii–iv.
10. James MacGregor Burns, *Uncommon Sense* (New York: Harper & Row, 1972), p. 53.
11. Cecil V. Crabb, Jr., *Bipartisan Foreign Policy: Myth or Reality?* (White Plains, N.Y.: Row, Peterson, 1957), pp. 241 and 245–46.
12. American Political Science Association, Committee on Political Parties, *Toward a More Responsible Two-Party System, American Political Science Review,* Supplement (1950), v. 44. p. 19.
13. Robert A. Dahl, *Congress and Foreign Policy* (n. 5, Chapter 2), p. 198.
14. *Executive-Legislative Communications,* Chapter 4.
15. Wilson, *Congressional Government* (Cleveland: Meridian Books, 1967), pp. 167–68. Originally published in 1885.
16. Samuel B. Huntington, "Congressional Responses to the Twentieth Century," in David B. Truman, ed., *The Congress and America's Future,* 2nd ed. (Englewood Cliffs: Prentice-Hall, 1973), pp. 6–38.
17. See Seymour Scher, "Conditions for Legislative Control," *Journal of Politics,* v. 25 (August, 1963), pp. 526–51.
18. Morris S. Ogul, *Congress Oversees the Bureaucracy* (Pittsburgh: University of Pittsburgh Press, 1976), esp. Chapters 1, 6, and 7.
19. See Roger H. Davidson, "Breaking Up Those 'Cozy Triangles': An Impossible Dream?", presented at the Symposium on Legislative Reform and Public Policy, University of Nebraska, Lincoln, Nebraska, March 11–12, 1976.
20. Lewis Anthony Dexter, "Congressmen and the Making of Military Policy," in Robert Peabody and Nelson W. Polsby, eds., *New Perspectives on the House of Representatives,* 2nd ed. (Chicago: Rand McNally, 1969), p. 181.
21. Lowi, "Making Democracy Safe for the World," *Domestic Sources,* p.

301. Emphasis in original. See also Schattschneider, *Party Government,* p. 8.

22. Contrast this argument to the one made by Waltz that democratic institutions in the United States *do not* hinder foreign policy decision-making; see Waltz, *Foreign Policy and Democratic Politics* (n. 15, Chapter 1), esp. Chapter 11.

23. See Richard Hofstadter, *The Idea of a Party System* (Berkeley: University of California Press, 1970), p. 68.

SUGGESTIONS FOR FURTHER READING

CHAPTER 1

HENKIN, LOUIS. *Foreign Affairs and the Constitution*. Mineola, N.Y.: Foundation Press, 1973.

LOWI, THEODORE J. "American Business, Public Policy, Case Studies, and Political Theory," *World Politics*, July, 1964.

MANNING, BAYLESS. "The Congress, the Executive and Intermestic Affairs: Three Proposals." *Foreign Affairs*, January 1977.

WILDAVSKY, AARON. "The Two Presidencies," *Trans-Action*, December, 1966.

CHAPTER 2

CAMPBELL, JOHN F. *The Foreign Affairs Fudge Factory*. New York: Basic Books, 1971.

FULBRIGHT, J. W. *The Crippled Giant*. New York: Random House, 1972.

HALPERIN, MORTON, *et al. The Lawless State*. Baltimore, Md.: Penguin Books, 1977. *The Pentagon Papers*. New York: Bantam Books, 1971.

PEPPERS, DONALD A. "The Two Presidencies: Eight Years Later," in Wildavsky, Aaron, ed. *Perspectives on the Presidency*. Boston: Little, Brown and Co., 1974.

SPANIER, JOHN. *American Foreign Policy Since World War II*, 6th edition. New York: Praeger Publishers, 1973.

CHAPTER 3

BAUER, RAYMOND A., *et al. American Business and Public Policy,* 2d edition. Chicago: Aldine-Atherton, 1972.

BERKOWITZ, MORTON, BOCK, P. G., and FUCCILLO, VINCENT J. *The Politics of American Foreign Policy.* Englewood Cliffs, N.J.: Prentice-Hall, 1977.

HALPERIN, MORTON H., and ARNOLD KANTER, eds. *Readings in American Foreign Policy: A Bureaucratic Perspective.* Boston: Little, Brown & Co., 1973.

HILSMAN, ROGER. *To Move a Nation.* New York: Doubleday & Co., 1967.

HUNTINGTON, SAMUEL P. *The Common Defense.* New York: Columbia University Press, 1961.

MUELLER, JOHN E. *War, Presidents and Public Opinion.* New York: John Wiley, 1972.

ROBINSON, JAMES A. *Congress and Foreign Policy,* revised edition. Homewood, Ill.: Dorsey Press, 1967.

ROSENAU, JAMES A., ed. *Domestic Sources of Foreign Policy.* New York: Free Press, 1967.

CHAPTER 4

ALLISON, GRAHAM. *Essence of Decision.* Boston: Little, Brown & Co., 1971.

DESTLER, I. M. *Presidents, Bureaucrats, and Foreign Policy.* Princeton, N.J.: Princeton University Press, 1972.

GALUCCI, ROBERT L. *Neither Peace Nor Honor.* Baltimore, Md.: The Johns Hopkins University Press, 1975.

HALPERIN, MORTON. "The Decision to Deploy the ABM: Bureaucratic and Domestic Politics in the Johnson Administration," *World Politics,* October, 1972.

———. *Bureaucratic Politics and Foreign Policy.* Washington, D.C.: The Brookings Institution, 1974.

LINDBLOM, CHARLES E. *The Intelligence of Democracy.* New York: Free Press, 1965.

RIPLEY, RANDALL B., and FRANKLIN, GRACE A. *Congress, the Bureaucracy, and Public Policy.* Homewood, Ill.: Dorsey, 1976.

CHAPTER 5

BURNS, JAMES MACGREGOR. *Uncommon Sense.* New York: Harper & Row, 1972.

CRABB, CECIL V., Jr. *Bipartisan Foreign Policy: Myth or Reality?* White Plains, N.Y.: Row, Peterson, & Co., 1957.

RANNEY, AUSTIN. *The Doctrine of Responsible Party Government.* Urbana: University of Illinois Press, 1962.

SCHLESINGER, ARTHUR M., Jr. *The Imperial Presidency.* Boston: Houghton Mifflin, 1973.

WALTZ, KENNETH N. *Foreign Policy and Democratic Politics.* Boston: Little, Brown & Co., 1966.

WILCOX, FRANCIS O. *Congress, the Executive and Foreign Policy.* New York: Harper & Row, 1971.

INDEX